The media's watching Vault! Here's a sampling of our coverage.

"For those hoping to climb the ladder of success, [Vault's] insights are priceless."
– ***Money magazine***

"The best place on the web to prepare for a job search."
– ***Fortune***

"[Vault guides] make for excellent starting points for job hunters and should be purchased by academic libraries for their career sections [and] university career centers."
– ***Library Journal***

"The granddaddy of worker sites."
– ***U.S. News and World Report***

"A killer app."
– ***New York Times***

One of Forbes' 33 "Favorite Sites"
– ***Forbes***

"To get the unvarnished scoop, check out Vault."
– ***Smart Money Magazine***

"Vault has a wealth of information about major employers and job-searching strategies as well as comments from workers about their experiences at specific companies."
– ***The Washington Post***

"Vault has become the go-to source for career preparation."
– ***Crain's New York Business***

"Vault [provides] the skinny on working conditions at all kinds of companies from current and former employees."
– ***USA Today***

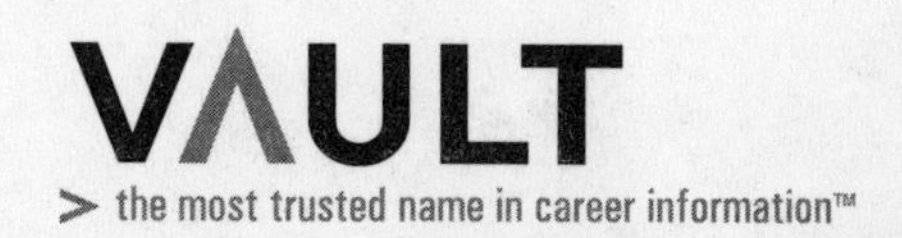

VAULT GUIDE TO SCREENWRITING CAREERS

VAULT GUIDE TO SCREENWRITING CAREERS

DAVID KUKOFF
AND THE STAFF OF VAULT

For information about permission to reproduce selections from this book, contact Vault Inc., 150 W. 22nd St., 5th Floor, New York, NY 10011, (212) 366-4212.

Library of Congress CIP Data is available.

ISBN 1-58131-370-5

Printed in the United States of America

ACKNOWLEDGMENTS

David Kukoff's acknowledgements:

I would like to thank Linda Venis and Brandon Gannon at UCLA Extension for providing me with a medium in which to proffer forth my opinions regarding the craft and business of screenwriting.

An additional thank you to Joel Fields, who made this book deal possible, as well as Marcy Lerner and Matthew Thornton at the Vault for their limitless patience and truly constructive criticism.

And the biggest thanks of all to my wife, Ilana, and children Zachary and Alexandra, who are the best stories my life has ever told.

Vault's acknowledgments:

We are extremely grateful to Vault's entire staff for all their help in the editorial, production and marketing processes. Vault also would like to acknowledge the support of our investors, clients, employees, family, and friends. Thank you!

Table of Contents

Chapter 5: Screenwriting Basics: Dialogue and Scene 55

GETTING HIRED 67

Chapter 6: Film Schools/Formal Screenwriting Programs 69

Chapter 7: Alternate Strategies for Getting In 77

ON THE JOB 85

Chapter 8: Agents for Screenwriters 87

Introduction

Storytelling through the ages

The urge to tell stories is as primitive an instinct as exists, and the desire to incorporate a visual component to one's storytelling dates all the way back to prehistoric man, whose engravings on stone walls brought his world alive for descendants thousand of years later. And although live theater has been a storytelling staple for centuries, the advent of film not only ushered in an entire new realm of visual possibilities (whose technical ceiling seems to rise to unforeseen new heights every decade) to represent stories both realistic and fantastic, but also created a medium for those stories to be consumed de-centrically – that is, away from the story's immediate location or social context, which qualified film as the first truly globally accessible medium.

Its impact can change a story's fortunes considerably; The *Lost Weekend* was a respectable novel by Charles R. Jackson, but it is the Academy Award-winning film version by Billy Wilder that is etched inexorably in the minds of people familiar with the property. Erin Brockovich certainly warranted her status as a good citizen based on her remarkable work against the Pacific Gas and Electric Company, but it wasn't until her story was brought to life as a Julia Roberts-starring (and notably, though not as publicly, Steven Soderbergh-directed, Susannah Grant-scripted) film that Ms. Brockovich's name became synonymous with the redemptive powers of improbable grass-roots triumph. And although television, whose business model is such that the goal is to create hundreds of episodic representations of its characters, has usurped film as mankind's premier global storytelling forum, there is something about film's ability to tell a self-contained story that makes it feel undeniably more human; just like people, each film is unique (sequels and remakes notwithstanding) – crafted and shaped just so. And the underlying basis for film, visually-driven medium though it may be, is the screenplay – the written word.

What is a screenplay?

Put simply, a screenplay is a blueprint for a movie. And just like an architectural blueprint, it can be quite technical: replete with camera shots, narrative, and stage direction, it can make the format a bit untenable for less-seasoned readers. Yet at the root of all the detailed action and would-be camera virtuosity lie the essential common denominators found in all storytelling mediums that, if executed well, break down the "fourth wall" and merge the viewer with the experience unfolding before his or her eyes. And with the public's increasing emphasis on and need for entertainment (the vast majority of American households view their cable bill as a utility) and overseas markets capable of revenue explosive enough to turn an underperformer into a bonanza (*Troy*, starring Brad Pitt, is an excellent example of a film that would not have been profitable were it not for its overseas grosses), the possibilities for writers to contribute to the lexicon of shared pop-cultural experiences have never been greater in number or available for so many.

Which means that if you've ever had a yen to write, to get your words and ideas heard by millions, now is the time.

But how? The landscape is puzzling and the craft is downright Sisyphean at times – one step forward, two steps back, especially in the beginning when you frequently feel like tossing everything but the brads holding the script together. What is important to remember, especially upon hearing phrases like "it's all who you know," is that while this can be true in any industry with regard to getting your foot in the door, becoming a professional screenwriter will require you to call upon vast reserves of craft and business savvy that can be learned; combine that with some actual talent and the possibilities of realizing your dream can be downright awe-inspiring.

Before you start scouring the earth for every contact within a degree or so of separation from someone in Hollywood, your first goal should be to write as many screenplays as possible and evaluate your progress by comparing it to professional-level scripts. Your next step, once you're satisfied with your work, is to write a commercially viable script on "spec" – speculatively, as opposed to writing for money upfront – and find an agent, manager, or combination of both to represent your script for sale. In selling a script you will not only be put in a position to be hired by studios and production companies to adapt books, plays, and other forms of source material into screenplays, you can also be considered to rewrite existing scripts that studios are unhappy with. Adaptations and rewrites are referred to as writing assignments; if you can receive enough assignments while continuing to sell your original material (which, as you become a more established writer, you can "pitch" without having to write upfront), you will have achieved your career goal of being a working screenwriter.

Keep in mind that selling a script is the best way to begin your career, but that you can still be considered for writing assignments without having done so-provided, of course, that the caliber of your work sufficiently impresses the studio and producer representatives in charge of maintaining the lists of writers with whom they are interested in working. Once you've gained entry, you should aim to make and maintain as many fans as possible at the studios and with simpatico producers (whose job it is to help sell scripts they are interested in producing to studios) so that you will continue to be considered for writing assignments-which you never want to do exclusive to your own work. It is important not to lose sight of the fact that you are still, at the end of the (pay) day, an artist who must remain true to developing your own stories and the voices that power them.

This is how most screenplay careers get launched. This book will give you the tools and advice you need to embark on this exciting journey. In the ensuing pages we will categorically address the building blocks of successful scripts and how to get your scripts made into movies, including:

- Why some stories are inherently well-suited for the big screen while others are not.
- The basic structural components of a script, and why certain choices, when properly implemented, can lead to its ultimate success.
- The "show, don't tell" philosophy and how it relates to film characters.
- The difference between dialogue and everyday conversation.
- What types of ideas studios tend to be looking for, and the commercial categories in which they fall.
- The steps you must take to turn a script sale into a writing career.
- How to make sense of the day-to-day operations of the entertainment industry – everything from the difference between managers and agents to the role of a producer to the high-turnover intensive hierarchy of the studio system.

As you read these pages, fully aware that there is no "magic bullet" for success in this profession, you will begin to identify patterns in the ways in which screen stories are told and will learn how to use these structural models and patterns to fit your own story's needs which, if consistent with those of the studios, will dramatically increase your chances of success in this industry.

VAULT CAREER GUIDES

ORGANIZED BY BOOK TYPE

VAULT CAREER TOPIC GUIDES	PRICE	PAGES	ISBN
The College Career Bible	9.95	402	1-58131-283
The MBA Career Bible	9.95	284	1-58131-284
Vault Guide to Top Internships	14.95	550	1-58131-291
Vault Guide to Resumes, Cover Letters and Interviews	19.95	138	1-58131-258
Vault Guide to Schmoozing	19.95	312	1-58131-205
Vault Guide to International Careers	19.95	196	1-58131-270
Vault Guide to Starting Your Own Business	19.95	176	1-58131-180
Vault Guide to Conquering Corporate America*	19.95	164	1-58131-178
The College Buzz Book	14.95	638	1-58131-297
The Business School Buzz Book	14.95	678	1-58131-295
The Law School Buzz Book	14.95	584	1-58131-296
Vault Guide to Finance Interviews	29.95	172	1-58131-304
Vault Guide to the Case Interview	29.95	144	1-58131-170

VAULT INDUSTRY CAREER GUIDES	PRICE	PAGES	ISBN
Vault Career Guide to Accounting	29.95	128	1-58131-328
Vault Career Guide to Advertising	29.95	114	1-58131-267
Vault Career Guide to Biotech	29.95	198	1-58131-26
Vault Career Guide to Book Publishing	29.95	140	1-58131-26
Vault Guide to Capitol Hill Careers	29.95	112	1-58131-25
Vault Guide to Corporate Law Careers	29.95	168	1-58131-22
Vault Career Guide to Consulting	29.95	184	1-58131-16
Vault Career Guide to the Energy Industry	29.95	176	1-58131-37
Vault Career Guide to the Fashion Industry	29.95	128	1-58131-20
Vault Guide to Flight Attendant Careers	29.95	160	1-58131-30
Vault Career Guide to Hedge Funds	29.95	144	1-58131-30
Vault Guide to Human Resources Careers	29.95	128	1-58131-36
Vault Career Guide to Interior Design	29.95	192	1-58131-32
Vault Career Guide to Investment Banking	29.95	152	1-58131-30
Vault Career Guide to Investment Management	29.95	128	1-58131-17
Vault Career Guide to Journalism and Information Media	29.95	208	1-58131-35
Vault Guide to Litigation Law Careers	29.95	168	1-58131-18
Vault Career Guide to Marketing & Brand Management	29.95	78	1-58131-13
Vault Career Guide to Media & Entertainment	29.95	152	1-58131-20
Vault Career Guide to Pharmaceutical Sales ('05)	29.95	128	1-58131-38
Vault Career Guide to Real Estate	29.95	120	1-58131-17
Vault Career Guide to Sales & Trading	29.95	160	1-58131-25
Vault Guide to Technology Careers	29.95	128	1-58131-37
Vault Career Guide to Venture Capital	29.95	128	1-58131-28

VAULT INDUSTRY EMPLOYER GUIDES	PRICE	PAGES	ISBN
Vault Guide to the Top 20 Accounting Firms	29.95	216	1-58131-31
Vault Guide to the Top Financial Services Employers	29.95	424	1-58131-26
Vault Guide to the Top 50 Banking Employers	29.95	560	1-58131-29
Vault Guide to Top Biotech/Pharmaceuticals Employers	19.95	182	1-58131-31
Vault Guide to the Top 50 Consulting Firms	29.95	598	1-58131-29
Vault Guide to the Top Consumer Products Employers	19.95	366	1-58131-32
Vault Guide to the Top Energy & Oil/Gas Employers	19.95	198	1-58131-31
Vault Guide to the Top Health Care Employers	29.95	424	1-58131-31
Vault Guide to the Top Insurance Employers	19.95	232	1-58131-3
Vault Guide to the Top 100 Law Firms	19.95	244	1-58131-35
Vault Guide to the Top 25 Tech Consulting Firms	19.95	166	1-58131-3
Vault Guide to the Top Tech Employers	39.95	768	1-58131-2
Vault Guide to the Top Telecom Employers	19.95	282	1-58131-3

THE SCOOP

Screenwriting Basics: Format

CHAPTER 1

Most screenwriters aren't simply movie buffs who hit it big; they're craftsmen and women who genuinely love the writing process and have mastered the technical details. Before getting down to the holy trinity of screenwriting – character, structure, and dialogue – you will need to know what a screenplay actually looks like and should know a bit about screenwriting software (it is highly recommended that you purchase one of the main scriptwriting programs, which will be discussed in a later chapter). Also, you should be reading as many actual screenplays as you can get your hands on, the most recent of which you can access via websites that publish shooting scripts from finished films (bookstores that feature scripts are also a good idea; however, they will most likely not be stocking an extensive collection).

Bear in mind while reading shooting scripts that you will not, in your script's initial stages, be called upon to include things like scene and shot numbers; the drafts you're reading were prepared with specific production notes that are never included in scripts without budget breakdowns. Still, even when writing a script on spec, it is important to remember that a screenplay does not exist for its own sake and thus must always be read with potential production considerations in mind; you will want to adopt certain visually evocative devices that will bring a sense of filmic flow to your script. Even prior to writing the words "fade in," however, you'll want to consider your outline and script length.

Outlining

An outline is a highly detailed synopsis of your script's story, written in bullet-point form that makes every key plot and character development abundantly clear. Outlines make good creative and pragmatic sense, for in addition to helping organize your thoughts and giving you a sense of your script's beginning, middle and end, you will be required to provide one when you are working on assignment for studios (which will be discussed further in later chapters). This isn't to say you won't deviate from it once it's time to write your script; you will. Extensively. But because organization is the key to economy, which itself – given the format's immense technical constraints – is a key component to writing a successful screenplay, it is a good idea to think of your story in terms of individual, two-dimensional scenes which you will then flesh out further when it comes time to write your script.

Unlike screenplays which, as earlier stated, adhere in structure and principle to certain specifications, there is no definitive way to write an outline. Every writer has his or her own preferred outlining method; whether or not you opt to number your scenes or incorporate act breaks (more on those later as well) is up to you. Given the lack of absolutes involved in outlining, however, as well as the overwhelming number of story and character ideas with which you must come up, outlining can sometimes prove even more daunting than writing the actual screenplay. Your finished outline should be anywhere from eight to twenty pages long, and should encompass all the information important to the story without including too much extraneous detail.

Below is a sample of how a professional outline looks. If you choose to divide your outline into three acts (and you probably should for your own organizational purposes at the very least), you should announce the act breaks in bold-faced, capital letters, like this:

ACT ONE

Then you should number or, if you are using Microsoft word, block out the scenes in which you will succinctly describe either the crucial character or plot elements (or both) that occur within the scene. Make sure you capitalize the names of all characters you introduce. Like this:

ACT ONE

1. Introduce SAM MILLER, late 30's, a private eye, as he works late in his office in New Orleans. From the looks of things, it's been a while since he's had a decent case.

2. Sam at home. Things pretty quiet around here as well; it could sure use a woman's touch. Maybe replace some of the empty pizza boxes and whiskey bottles with flowers and doilies.

3. Sam asleep later that night. The phone rings. In a half-drunk stupor, he answers it. Hears a WOMAN'S VOICE, telling him to be in his office in a half hour. Click…

What you don't want to do is include too much exposition (aka: needless details) that isn't relevant to the plot or characters. For example, with regard to the second paragraph above, you would want to avoid something like the bold-faced phrase below, which would definitely qualify as exposition…

1. Sam at home. Things pretty quiet around here as well; it could sure use a woman's touch. Maybe replace some of the empty pizza boxes and whiskey bottles with flowers and doilies. **Sam's couch is brown, and his dining room table is white.**

… unless it was modified with something like this:

1. Sam at home. Things pretty quiet around here as well; it could sure use a woman's touch. Maybe replace some of the empty pizza boxes and whiskey bottles with flowers and doilies. **Sam's couch is brown** with a spring that's probably ready to pop just below the couch's threadbare surface, **and his dining room table is white** and looks like it was purchased as an afterthought.

These modifications tell us more about Sam's character; we know that he is either poor, neglectful, or both, and his mannerisms and speech patterns will probably reflect the kind of man we would envision living in an environment like this.

As important as it is that your outline be succinct, however, you should be mindful not to make it feel too freeze-dried either; the goal is to try to make your reader feel as though he has just finished a great short story.

Page Count

Unlike a novel or other forms of fiction, screenplays have definite length requirements. The basic formula dictates that each page represents about a minute of screen time, and since most movies run between a hundred minutes and two hours, your script should (with very few exceptions) be between 100-120 pages and should always be paginated. Occasionally a family film or a broad comedy might run a bit shorter than 100 pages, and if you are writing an historical epic or a biographical script (known in the industry as a "biopic") there is a good chance that you will exceed the 120 page benchmark. But keep in mind that the first thing readers do when they pick up a script is flip to the back page to see how much work lies ahead of them. You never want to start off on the wrong foot by having the reader think to herself, "A hundred and thirty pages, huh? If I'm going to miss 'The Simpsons' for this, it had better be good."

Title Pages

Before you write the first page of your script, you should format a title page (all screenwriting softwares include this as part of the program). This is the page that acts as a kind of book cover, stating the script's title and who it's written by. It should look like this:

MY TITLE

By

My Name

There's no need to get fancy and write something like *An Original Screenplay* by (my name) – most readers assume this to begin with. The only time you'll need to add something to the format above is if the script is based on a true story or on a piece of source material, at which point you'd write:

MY TITLE

By

My Name

Based on the novel *TITLE*, by Author

You should then scroll down to the bottom right hand corner of the page and write your contact information – your street address, phone number (or numbers, if you wish to include your cell) and e-mail address. Once you've written your title page, it's time to turn the page over and start writing your script.

Getting started

The screenplay officially begins, in virtually every instance, with the following words at the exact page location as they appear below:

FADE IN:

These two words are always capitalized and are always followed by a colon. Most screenwriting software is trained to recognize these words and will automatically capitalize them when they are typed in.

Scene Headings and Narrative

A scene heading, which is also capitalized (and not, contrary to television formatting, underlined), describes where the action is taking place – interior or exterior – and offers an estimation as to what time of day the action is occurring. Placed two lines below the words "FADE IN" (or below the last line of the previous scene; some people and software use three lines), your scene heading will look something like this:

INT. SUPERMARKET – DAY

This lets the reader know the following:

- that the ensuing scene takes place in a supermarket
- that it is an interior shot (INT.)
- and that it occurs sometime during the day.

Some writers are more specific about the time of day in which the scene takes place, but this is generally not advised unless you have a good dramatic reason for it. Scene headings are always simply interior or exterior (INT. or EXT.), abbreviated, and in capital letters.

Let's say you want your character to be in two separate but adjoining locations (one exterior, one interior) and have him move immediately from one of these locations to another. For example, your character is going to run up the driveway to a house and go inside, then slowly make his way through that house. You would write two separate scene headings, the first of which would look something like this:

EXT. PROTAGONIST'S HOME – DAY

Then, after the character had gone inside:

INT. PROTAGONIST'S HOME – CONTINUOUS

The capitalized word "CONTINUOUS" informs the reader that, although you have broken up the scene into two different locations, you intend for the action to continue without a significant break in the film's timeline.

Once you have established the where and when of the action, you are now officially inside the scene. Sometimes, though, before you address what your characters are actually doing or saying within that scene, you'll want to create the atmosphere where the scene takes place; this will not only make the script more visual for the reader, it will additionally give the scene its overall timbre. This device is called narration and is usually denoted by a non-indented single-spaced sentence or small paragraph two lines below the scene heading. Say for example you wanted to have your characters pull up in front of a creepy house. You could establish both the action of the car pulling up and the foreboding feeling the house gives off by writing:

EXT. BAYOU HOUSE – DAY

A murky, haunted place whose jaundiced corners cut the occasional sharp angle through the omnipresent, watery fog.

Well-written narrative is enjoyable to read and can be an almost novelistic tool that brings your settings to life.

Dialogue

Once you've established the overall setting and ambience of the scene, it's time to let your characters say what they must in order to move your story along. The characters' names and their dialogue should appear, proportionally, in the middle of the page, not near the page's left margin.

JOE

You scared of what's inside?

HELEN

Inside what? You or that creepy house?

Dialogue should run roughly to the margins as indicated above, is always single-spaced and follows the same grammatical rules as any other form of prose.

Transitions

A popular misconception shared by novice screenwriters is that every scene must end with a transition (a "CUT TO" or "DISSOLVE TO" – always capitalized) prior the next scene heading.

HELEN

Let's get out of here!

Joe and Helen run out of the house, just inches ahead of the shots that are fired after them.

CUT TO:

INT. JOE'S CAR – DAY

Joe and Helen drive along, still shaking from their experience.

JOE

What the hell was that?

Although this tended to be the case in older formatted screenplays, the current model favors going directly from the end of a scene to the next scene heading.

HELEN

Let's get out of here!

Joe and Helen run out of the house, just inches ahead of the shots that are fired after them.

INT. JOE'S CAR – DAY

Joe and Helen drive along, still shaking from their experience.

JOE

What the hell was that?

This is not to say that transitions are not still used; indeed, sometimes a "CUT TO" can give the reader a more immediate sense of urgency or quickness in spilling over from one scene to the next. For example, let's say that you would like to end your scene on an especially filmic image, a visual segue that will lead your reader seamlessly into the next scene. Even though most scenes start with a scene heading, you'd like to give the reader a good jolt. You would therefore dispense with the scene heading and begin the next scene with a close-up or a shot that conveys the very next image that we would be seeing onscreen. It would look something like this:

Joe and Helen's eyes GO WIDE. For sitting there, right in front of them, is none other than Helen's "dead" father.

PUSH IN on the cigarette smoke unfurling from the butt in the ashtray and…

CUT TO:

A CLOUD OF FOG

as it rolls over the swamp.

Writing a new scene heading in this case would convey the message that the scene previous had ended and might thus break the tension; in the example given, you would suck the reader right into the next scene with a visual and without a warning, which makes the script more exciting and filmic. And the more filmic and visceral you can make the reading experience for the person reading it, the better your chances of having that reader march the script into his superior's office and insist that she read it right away.

The "CUT TO" transition can also be used to comic effect as well. Take the case of two parents sitting in the sun, enjoying the first vacation they've had from their teenaged twin sons in years. The father could see the mother's concerned expression and urge her to relax, adding:

DAD

Marge, they're fifteen years old. What's the worst thing they could do?

CUT TO:

DAD'S FERRARI

as it ZOOMS down the block, the blissful shrieks of innocent, fifteen year-old MEGAN and SUSAN all but disappearing amidst the SQUEAL of the car's rubber tires.

The "DISSOLVE TO" transition (which appears in the same place as the "CUT TO" transition) usually denotes a passage of time – anything from days to months – and tends to be used less than the "CUT TO" transition. Often it is used in conjunction with a montage, another device that helps move time forward.

DISSOLVE TO:

MONTAGE

Where we see, in succession:

- Megan and Susan cruising through the suburban streets of Bloomfield Hills at top speeds, BLOWING away virtually every model of every car GM has ever manufactured.

- The girls finishing up dinner in an upscale restaurant, Megan not so much as batting an eye as she plunks down Dad's plastic on the bill.

- The Ferrari parked in front of Detroit's skankiest hip-hop club.

Now you have told the story of an entire day's worth of mischief in less than a third of a page. Although one hundred-plus pages might seem like a great deal of space, you will be surprised how far some good economical thinking and writing will go.

Camera Shots

In one of the above examples, the phrase "PUSH IN ON" was used. Capitalized directions like this are known as camera shots which, even though the movie has yet to be filmed, give the reader a greater sense of cinematic movement. The conventional wisdom may be that while readers of fiction might want to maintain their own vision for what the book's universe looks like (and indeed, many filmed adaptations of novels have failed due to this very reason), readers of screenplays realize that they are evaluating a blueprint and are thus better prepared for the movie to be brought to life by the work's author. Camera shots are always capitalized, placed in the body of the narrative description, and include items on the order of:

- PULL BACK TO REVEAL, or WIDEN TO REVEAL: Usually used in conjunction with a close up, after which we "pull back to reveal" the context in which the close up takes place.
- PAN OVER TO, or DOLLY OVER TO: Denotes a tracking camera shot, one where the camera is moving to the side of a visual, invariably to end on something of significance.
- ZOOM IN ON: Self-explanatory. Use only when you're pretty certain it's warranted; many writers have garnered unintentional laughs by zooming in on something that didn't shock or surprise a reader in the least.

While camera shots can be tremendous assets in making a story come to life, they should only be used when you feel it is absolutely necessary. And if you don't think one is absolutely necessary, it is generally better not to use it. Still, even though it is a widely acknowledged and accepted fact that the first thing a director does when he or she receives a script is cross out all the camera shots, you should be in no way deterred from using them to make the script a more enjoyable read.

Isolation shots

Let's say you'd like to emphasize a particular visual. You don't want to use "CUT TO" since that would connote a new scene entirely. What you can do is isolate the shot within the scene.

Joe and Helen turn around slowly. Can't bear to look. But finally do. And are horrified to see…

A SKELETON
standing right behind them.

What this does is tell the reader that the object or visual denoted in capitals will be the subject of its very own shot.

Screenwriting Software

The good news about everything you've just read is that you don't really have to format it yourself. Because screenwriting is a technical craft that requires a great deal of visual configuration, writers pre-computer often found themselves spending as much time tabbing and editing margins as actually creating the magic that was supposed to lie within them.

As a result, software like Final Draft, Scriptware, and Movie Magic (among others) was created. In taking care of the technical aspects of screenwriting, they leave the writer free to focus all their time on being creative. None of the software choices are difficult to use, and if you don't live near a specialty software store or university you can download an order form via a quick Internet engine search. Software tends to run anywhere from one hundred to two hundred dollars, and although Final Draft is the most commonly used brand, the others are easily imported into its format. Don't be fooled by software that claims to assist in the selection of story choices; as long as science fiction remains fiction, screenwriting software is a secretary, not a collaborator.

Reading Screenplays

You should be reading as many scripts as possible. Scripts in the active development stage are a difficult thing to come by in the entertainment industry; although copies occasionally make the rounds for work and research purposes, the studios and producers that control them are often wary of releasing their secrets to the world at large for various fears that range from paranoid to karmic in nature. Thus the best way to get to read the most current drafts of the most current scripts is to have a friend on the inside of an agency, management or production company, or studio, or to know a journalist who is doing an entertainment-related piece and can lend you his copy of the script to the movie on which he happens to be reporting. You should try to read any script you can get your hands on, even if it doesn't involve subject matter that you could see yourself someday writing; the point is to get as familiar as possible with what professional writing looks and sounds like and to try to get your own writing as close in quality to that of writers who do this for a living. Simply reading a well-written script will help you get used to the rhythms you should aim to emulate.

If you cannot get to anyone on the inside of the studios, however, there's always the option of downloading finished, shooting scripts from the websites www.screenplay.com and www.scriptorama.com. Both sites stock a wide selection and are relatively user-friendly. You should download scripts frequently and read as many as you possibly can; in addition to containing everything you will ever need to know about style and formatting, finished screenplays (even the ones that fall well short of *Chinatown*) are a veritable font of writing tips and will be instrumental in helping you develop your own writing style.

Screenwriting Basics: The Idea

CHAPTER 2

So far we've examined the nuts and bolts of drafting a script. But without the right idea driving it, your script will never see celluloid. Because if the screenplay is the blueprint to the film – the two-dimensional planning plane from which the three-dimensional images ultimately spring forth – then the one-dimensional, amoeba-like speck at the origin of the film's evolution would be the core idea or premise. And although writers do often sell scripts on the basis of the material's timeliness or extraordinary writing, the vast majority of the projects that sell to studios are idea-driven. And the most tantalizing ideas to studio executives tend to be the ones that fall under the category of "high concept."

The High-Concept Idea

A high concept is usually defined as an idea that can be explained in one sentence and gives you the gist of the entire movie. For example, *Bruce Almighty* could be summed-up in the following pitch line: a frustrated reporter, who's angry with God, receives His powers for a week. Not only do you understand the underlying basis of the movie from that one line, you also see why it could potentially be funny even before you're told that Jim Carrey will be playing the newly-deified mortal. Another example: a teenager gets to wreak havoc on the lives of his parents when they were his age, courtesy of a time machine (*Back To The Future*, a structural analysis of which will be covered in a later section). Again, we are now well-aware that we're in for a doozy of a ride – literally, in the case of the film's protagonist, who will get to experience the universal teenage fantasy of seeing what his parents were like as teenagers.

As evidenced by these two models, there is often an otherworldly or magical component in high-concept films; a suspension of disbelief, however, is hardly a prerequisite. Witness the example set by the movie *Seven*, in which a serial killer is doing away with his victims via grotesque interpretations of the seven deadly sins. With this one sentence it is clear not only what the movie is about, but also what its tone and overall theme will be.

Below are more examples of high-concept ideas and their possible accompanying pitch lines:

- *50 First Dates*: A shameless womanizer falls in love with a short-term amnesiac, thus forcing him to woo her every day of their courtship.

- *The Truman Show*: A man finds out that his entire life is a television show.

- *Hide And Seek*: A widower's daughter invents an imaginary friend that starts to kill people.

- *Bringing Down The House*: A lawyer requests to meet a woman with whom he's been corresponding online… only to realize that she's a prisoner who broke out of jail to meet him.

- *Twisted*: A female detective comes to the chilling realization that all the victims of the serial killer she's investigating were ex-boyfriends of hers.

While high-concept ideas don't always translate into spec sales – and the ones that do sell and get made aren't always hits, especially true in the case of the last title listed above – studio executives and producers tend to have an easier time seeing how the movie can be quickly explained to audiences through print ads and trailers. In fact, some executives have been known to say that if they can't envision the trailer they simply won't buy the script.

A good way to determine whether or not your idea is high-concept is to try to figure out a one or two-line hook on the order of the ones listed above. Then sit back and ask yourself, based on that hook, the following questions:

- Do I get where the movie's basic plot is headed?

- Do I understand why it will be funny/scary/sad?

- Do I know the overall tone?

If the answer is "yes," then chances are you are well on your way to writing a high-concept script.

Case Study

Robert Kosberg, King of the High Concept

Robert Kosberg, the producer of movies such as the mind-warping *12 Monkeys* as well as more conventional fare like the shark thriller *Deep Blue Sea*, is a veritable high-concept pitch cottage industry. Kosberg, who generates story ideas with writers and then remains on the project as a producer, has pitched and sold ideas such as *Surrender, Dorothy* which hypothesizes that the Wicked Witch of the West never died, but rather had been in an Oz jail all those years; now she's out and coming after the adult Dorothy for her slippers (Drew Barrymore was at one point attached to the project). Kosberg loves inversions of classic tales – Shakespeare is a treasure trove of material ripe for reinvention – because of their high recognizability factor, but welcomes ideas from all genres (although he does confess to be somewhat partial to comedies as they tend to generate the most immediate response).

Kosberg likes to trace back the origins of high-concept fare to executives like Barry Diller and Michael Eisner who would later, respectively, become the heads of the Fox network and the Walt Disney Studios. Diller and Eisner created and programmed ABC's hugely successful movie-of-the-week (M.O.W.) genre in the mid-1970s. They noticed that millions of people would read the two-line description of the movie in TV Guide and base whether they tuned in or not on the idea alone. Given the ubiquity – yea, saturation levels – of news stories concerning film and television properties in our daily lives, a film with an easily-digestible high-concept pitch line is more likely to attract attention.

Kosberg is not only a prolific originator of high-concept hooks, he also sponsors several competitions that seek out other similarly conceived ideas for movies. Kosberg believes that there are far more great story ideas than there are great screenplays but advises beginning screenwriters not to fall in love with the first high-concept idea they cook up. Instead, try and come up with as many of these ideas as possible. Test them out on co-workers, family members, and anyone else who professes to be a moviegoer, the point being to see if people not only get the movie but also like the idea. The best ideas do often sell, and the writer who generated the idea can negotiate at least the first draft. More often than not, that will be the beginning and end of your involvement in the project, but Kosberg is living proof that if you can generate the ideas, the doors will always be open.

Blank Meets Blank

An additional exercise that will help you determine the high-concept viability of your script is to think of two movies that your script resembles. Then try to envision your script as a merging of elements from those two films, so that the summation of your script idea would be *Movie A* meets *Movie B*. For example, a comedy about a dead body that comes back to life and haunts a crazy, hormonally-driven high school could be summed up as *Weekend at Bernie's* meets *Fast Times at Ridgemont High*, two movie references that manage to marry a specific script component – in this case the dead body – with a specific atmosphere, creating the havoc that will yield a movie. A thriller about a cannibalistic serial killer who targets only the most beautiful young women in town could be pitched as *The Silence of the Lambs* meets *Kiss the Girls*. Again, the conceit of a serial killer antihero – in this case, one with a distinct forbearer – is evoked along with the nature of who he will be victimizing. An especially outrageous version of the *Blank* meets *Blank* process is on display in Robert Altman's hilarious Hollywood satire *The Player*, in which Tim Robbins' studio executive entertains pitch after pitch, including one whose writers manage to sum up their pitch as *Pretty Woman* meets *Out of Africa*.

To get the hang of this exercise, examine a handful of movies that you would consider to be high-concept and figure out a way to pitch them as *Blank* meets *Blank*. Then, try to replicate this process as often as possible when seeing movies (or even print ads) in the future. The following recently released films are good examples of how the *Blank* meets *Blank* paradigm can be applied to virtually anything.

- *Kicking and Screaming*, with Will Ferrell, could be pitched as *The Big Green* meets *Nothing In Common* (kids' soccer meets troubled father/son relationship).
- *Hitch* could be pitched as *Alfie* meets *How To Lose A Guy In Ten Days* (charming cad meets untenable romantic situation for which he's not prepared).
- *Sin City* could be pitched as *Pulp Fiction* meets *Cool World* (violent fractured narrative about hoods meets cool, half-animated universe).
- *Sideways* could be pitched as *Diner* meets *Two For The Road* (male bonding meets road trip with unpredictable results).

- *Eurotrip* could be pitched as *American Pie* meets *National Lampoon's European Vacation* (teenage sex hijinks combined with the Ugly Americans abroad).
- *Mr. and Mrs. Smith* could be pitched as *Prizzi's Honor* meets *True Lies* (hit man spouses combined with a domestic situation that is far more than meets the eye).
- *Cinderella Man* could be pitched as *Rocky* meets *Brother, Can You Spare A Dime?* (underdog boxer combined with a Depression-era situation).

And If It Isn't High-Concept?

Even though your best bet is to write a film that adheres to high-concept principles, there are certainly numerous examples of scripts that have sold that took a more low-concept (or no concept) approach. Sometimes the characters are simply so memorable and well-written that studio executives simply can't forget them, as was the case with the script for *Beautiful Girls*. Even though the subsequent movie didn't quite capture the same magic that had captivated industry readers, the script was passed around as a model of great character writing; the script's writer, Scott Rosenberg, soon shot to the top of the A-List and wrote several subsequent hit movies.

Character-driven fare, if well-written, also tends to have something of a shelf life even if it does not sell originally as a spec script; a good, tenacious producer, if she really believes in the material, will continue to contact managers and talent in the hopes of attaching an element (an actor or director with whom the studio wishes to be in business) and thus ushering the script into the development pool through the back door.

Genre

Provided you do decide to go the high-concept route, you now need to decide what kind of response you want to elicit from your readers and, ideally, viewers. Do you want them to laugh, cry, squirm in their seats, or do all of the above? Much of this will be determined by what type of script you decide to write, as set forth by the following movie genres, or categories that movies tend to fall into. Genre is also important to understand from a commercial standpoint; just as no fast food restaurant would serve only hamburgers, studios feel the need to offer up a variety of movies that appeal to all ages and sensibilities:

1. **Comedy:** As self-explanatory a category as they come, comedy is the realm of the laugh. The genre of comedy is often sub-categorized into areas such as romantic comedy that invariably is centered around the "boy meets, loses, then gets girl" model (*Working Girl*, *Two Weeks Notice*); broad comedy that relies upon a good degree of physical humor (*Meet the Parents*, *Dodgeball*); or family comedy that is geared to please both adults as well as children (*The Incredibles*, *Men In Black*). As the saying goes in the industry, "funny is money." A further plus in writing a comedic script is that comedies are often the most popular specs on the market due to their high commercial appeal and lack of competition from other source material (plays, novels, video games, etc.) Which is not to say that movies don't occasionally spring from TV shows (*The Brady Bunch*, *Fat Albert*) or Saturday Night Live characters (*Wayne's World*, *A Night At The Roxbury*), but a dearth of comic novels, plays, and video games means that source material-based films tend to happen with far less frequency in comedy than in other genres.

2. **Drama:** This genre is something of a catch-all phrase for scripts that are driven more by character interaction than by plot. Many, if not most films that qualify as dramas derive from source material other than spec scripts: adaptations of fictional material (*The Hours*, *We Don't Live Here Anymore*), plays (*Closer*, *Finding Neverland*) or true-life stories (*Ray*, *Coach Carter*). Drama is considered the hardest genre to break into via spec script – mostly due to the reasons listed above – but a great writing sample can put you on the studios' radar for one of these writing assignments, and writing assignments are the key to longevity.

3. **Thriller:** Films that qualify as thrillers tend to be heavily plot-driven pieces that involve hair-raising twists and turns (*Seven*, *Taking Lives*). With the exception of the supernatural thriller sub-genre (*Constantine*, *Gothika*), this genre has fallen from grace somewhat due to several high-profile box office disappointments. The legal thriller sub-genre in particular, despite 2003's well-made *Runaway Jury*, has all but been banished to television and cable.

4. **Horror:** This genre encompasses everything from slasher and creature features (*Saw*, *Boogeyman*) to remakes of spooky Japanese movies (*The Ring*, *The Grudge*) to video game adaptations (*Resident Evil*). For those who don't mind the gore and splatter aspects and have a gift for turning peoples' stomachs, these films can be immensely enjoyable – not to

mention financially rewarding – to write. Worth keeping in mind: when looking to purchase horror spec scripts, most studios today are looking to buy "elegant" horror movies on the order of *The Others* or "cool" horror movies like *28 Days Later* rather than the standard slasher flicks like *Friday the 13th* or *Child's Play* (despite their venerability and profitability, they are not often purchased by studios due to a somewhat paradoxical-seeming sense of snobbery).

5. **Action:** Films of this genre tend to be driven by set-pieces (trailer-worthy, action-packed sequences) that test the limits of a writer's visual imagination. In the 1980s, action films were packing the multiplexes, thanks largely to stars like Arnold Schwarzenegger (*The Terminator*), Bruce Willis (*Die Hard*), and Sylvester Stallone (*Rambo*) whose films frequently turned into sequel-stacked franchises. A word of caution to the would-be action writer: a combination of the increasing age (or political aspirations) of these stars combined with audiences' need for more sophisticated fare (a la *The Matrix*) has led to a decline in the genre's viability, making the days of Shane Black selling *The Last Boy Scout* for four million dollars feel like a quaint (and enviable) distant memory.

6. **Science Fiction:** The science fiction genre (or, as it's commonly known, "sci-fi") is usually marked by a preponderance of futuristic technology at the service of a story that, despite its seemingly alien landscape, is really a metaphor for the human condition. A film like *I, Robot*, lulls us into thinking that it takes place so far in the future that it couldn't possibly have anything to do with current society until we realize that the themes – free will and what it truly means to be human – are every bit as pertinent today as they most likely will be in the future. The only problem with writing a science-fiction spec script is that there is so much existing fiction in this genre that most studios will simply option the book and hire writers to adapt them. A well-written science-fiction spec, however, can certainly land you on the list of writers to be considered for these assignments.

7. **Hybrids, or cross-genre films:** Sometimes writers decide to blend genres together. The results can be often be downright delightful and, in some cases, can even define a new subset category. For example, Diane Thomas – in whose honor an annual award is given at UCLA, where she attended nighttime screenwriting classes – decided that she'd never before seen a fulfilling blend of action and romantic comedy, and thus *Romancing The Stone* was born. Likewise, the 1980's film *48 Hours*, starring Nick Nolte and Eddie Murphy, spawned the beginning of what would become a string of buddy action films. Perhaps the most successful example of a film that combined several genres would be *Ghost*, which manages to be a

supernatural romantic thriller with significant comic overtones. Sometimes writers bite off more than they can chew; witness films like *I Heart Huckabees* (written and directed by David O. Russell, who had performed similar duties on the George Clooney/Mark Wahlberg/Ice Cube film *Three Kings*) which attempted to be an existentialist comic mystery. Still, if you feel strongly about combining mystery with, say, the musical, then by all means write it even if there is no existing precedent. You might just create a new model for future writers.

Pixar, Dreamworks and the Rise of the Computer-Animated Family Comedy

With the arrival of *Snow White and the Seven Dwarves*, the first-ever fully-feature length animated film, the Walt Disney Studios ushered in an era in which it enjoyed a veritable lock on animated family fare. Other studios attempted to break Disney's stranglehold on animation – which could be especially lucrative once ancillary revenue from toys and other related merchandise was factored in – but had no luck. One studio even screened the same film for two test audiences, once with the Disney logo and once with their own, only to find that the screening with the Disney logo scored much higher. Such was the power of the Disney brand name.

But in the late 1990s, two things happened. A company called Pixar, which self-funded its films but released them in theaters through Disney's distribution outlets, made an enormous splash with *Toy Story*, a film whose combination of sophisticated wit and technical wizardry dazzled audiences. Then a year later, DreamWorks (which had been co-founded by Jeffrey Katzenberg, the executive credited with pulling Disney out of a brief slump with fare such as *The Little Mermaid* and *Aladdin*), released *The Prince of Egypt* which, though not a huge hit, announced the arrival of another player on the scene. Since then, hand-drawn animation – last seen in box-office disappointments such as *Sinbad* and *Home on the Range* – has fallen out of favor, and studios like Fox and Sony have announced their desire to enter the lucrative world of computer animation.

What does this mean for you as a writer? Simply put, a chance to get a toehold in this imaginative market in which some of the best original screenplays are being written – witness the almost yearly Academy Award nomination in this category to the creative minds behind Pixar. The splitting-up of the pie is tantamount to the dissolution of the phone company, when baby Bells, Sprint, and MCI finally got their chance to take on the stalwart monopolist AT&T. More buyers means more opportunities for writers: Pixar recently announced the end of its business association with Disney, which means that Disney will have to work twice as hard to generate product with the Disney brand name.

As with every aspect of the entertainment industry, it is unlikely that you'll be an overnight success. Computer animation is costly, the films take years to complete, and some companies prefer to develop their films in-house. But new animation companies are sprouting up every day, buoyed by the increasing demand for cutting-edge animated fare, and the need for spec scripts in this genre has never been higher (plus a great writing sample could always put you in the running for a rewrite of an existing script or an adaptation of an optioned book or video game). So for the writer who, after a lifetime of Disney classics, remains a child at heart, or for the writer who has young children and would love to be a creative force behind something they would enjoy, these films represent an exciting career possibility.

Studio vs. "Indie" Films

In the course of the past ten years, the film business has been witness to an explosion of what are commonly known as "art house" films – movies that don't fit the traditional multiplex definition, and are frequently driven by smaller concepts and more complex character interaction. This model of film is hardly anything new; the modern-day "Golden Era" of the 1960s and 1970s saw a crop of European-influenced directors like Peter Bodganovich working within the studio and writer-directors such as John Cassavetes and John Sayles making films outside of it. However, the success of companies such as Miramax and Lion's Gate has served as sufficient encouragement to the major studios to back the production of smaller films like *Before Sunset* and *American Splendor*, whose budgets and economic model would have been unfathomable as recently as 10 years ago. And some films like *Monster*, due to the brave performances of their lead actors (in this case Charlize Theron, whose unrecognizable turn as the flipped-out, sun-scarred Aileen Wuornos earned her an Oscar) actually bring in a hefty profit along with their Academy Award nominations, which additionally earns the studio favor in the eyes of movie stars who, despite their reputations, do for the most part want to work on quality films.

Keep in mind, however, that even though some of these films ultimately make it into bigger theaters and are financed and developed by studio-backed specialty outfits, the business model these films present bears little resemblance to that of the big-budget films the studios release every year. The comparison is akin to a first-time novelist's small literary novel that is issued by a major publisher who will also publish the memoirs of Hillary Rodham Clinton during the same fiscal year. You must also keep in mind that although films like these frequently launch the careers of the writers involved, few people aside from the Coen Brothers and Alexander Payne make a living writing them; for starters, those writers also direct the films in question, which pays them more than their writing fees, and Payne – along with his writing partner, Jim Taylor, tends to supplement his income from small films with lucrative studio writing assignments on which his name rarely, if ever, appears. Because the simple truth is that the pay scale in smaller movies is commensurate with their budgets; which is to say far lower than studio fare, and these types of films don't involve hiring writers on assignment. But for the writer who, at least initially, sees him or herself writing on a smaller scale, what these films can provide is a produced credit, an entrée into the industry, and the possibility of directing a smaller, lower-risk project of your own.

Screenwriting Basics: Character

CHAPTER 3

So now that you've come up with your story idea, you must figure out how to populate it. Defining your characters is one of the most difficult tasks a screenwriter has to face; to wit, several books have been written about this very topic alone. The very notion of a hero – his or her quest and the obstacles he or she must overcome – has been a paradigm of folklore and mythology from Aristotle to Oliver Stone. To begin, there are some fundamental questions you must ask yourself: who would be the best possible character (or characters) to put your story into play? What kinds of noble (or ignoble) attributes do they embody? And who is trying to prevent them from realizing their goals? Who should be either rooting them along – or double-crossing them – as a member of the supporting cast, and how extensive should that supporting cast be?

The best place to start answering these questions is by identifying who your protagonist (main character or hero) and antagonist (main foil or obstacle – usually the villain) are. Although several movies employ an ensemble cast (*Diner*, *St. Elmo's Fire*, *Sideways*) in which there exists no one protagonist or antagonist, for the purposes of your first screenplay it would be best to focus on a story that does clearly define these roles. Once you have a firmer grasp on the rules and principles of screenwriting, you will discover unlimited ways to shape and develop complex, intriguing characters.

The Protagonist

The protagonist is, for lack of a better word, the hero of your movie. And although film history is replete with protagonists who have displayed ambiguous, even non-heroic character traits, we will assume that your protagonist is the good guy for the time being. What kinds of qualities can you give your protagonist to help shape the quest to fulfill her basic needs, and to what ultimate end? The following sections address the basic components of a protagonist, and offer examples of certain attributes which are typically necessary in order to create satisfying, richly-textured characters.

Motivation

People in the movies act very much the same as their counterparts in real life; otherwise, they would not be so relatable as to foster the suspension of disbelief required to hold an audience's attention. But in real life we tend find ourselves conflicted – in some cases, permanently – and unresolved, whereas in the movies this is simply not an option. So as screenwriters we ask ourselves: what makes for a satisfying ending? The answer? Resolution, which tends to occur when someone has been through a journey and achieved its end goal. This means that before you so much as type the words "Fade In", you must figure out what is motivating your character. And the motivation behind your protagonist's actions can be summed up by one simple question: what does he or she want – or need? Not necessarily in a material sense (although greed is as time-tested and easily understood a motivation as has ever existed), but rather from an emotional standpoint. Thus motivation can best be explained as an emotion that drives the protagonist and, by extension, propels the plot forward. For example, a man wrongly accused of a crime who is sent to a maximum security prison for life wants freedom; thus the plot of the movie entails his attempts to break out of jail. An idealistic district attorney who gets the opportunity to prosecute a sixty-five year-old Klansman for a bombing that killed five teenagers forty years prior wants justice; the film's plot will therefore detail her efforts to convict the man.

Character arc

Most protagonists begin a movie fairly incomplete; the events of the film therefore transpire in a way so as to put the character through the requisite steps he must follow to become whole and triumphant by the film's conclusion. The journey any character takes in a movie is known as his "character arc," which is thus named for the invisible, sloping arc that transports a character from origin point to completion point. If a character is well-meaning but selfish, that character's arc would most likely entail a series of events that would transform her into a giving person. If a character is an incorrigible ladies' man who, deep down, truly fears commitment, he might become involved in a relationship that proves to be long-term by the end of the movie. Keep in mind that a character's arc need not always yield a happy ending, just a necessary one; witness the journey of Julia Roberts' character in *My Best Friend's Wedding*, in which, eager to separate her friend from his fiancee, our protagonist descends upon the festivities determined to wreck the wedding, then realizes that she is the one who must ultimately let go. In the end she doesn't get the guy – bold terrain indeed for a romantic comedy – but she does come to an important realization about what's behind her jealousy, and winds up a more resolved character than she was at the movie's beginning, thus providing a satisfying experience for all involved.

Backstory

A "backstory" is a storytelling device that depicts the character's past prior to the movie's point of entry. Backstory is not the same thing as motivation, although often it can help explain why the protagonist is motivated to undergo the film's essential journey. Therefore the movie's beginning is not necessarily where the story begins; when we meet our protagonists they are usually at a point in their lives when they are reaching critical mass – something is about to happen that will force them to take actions that will change their lives forever. Say, for example, we decide to tell the story of a former convict who is forced to return to a life of crime in order to make ends meet. His backstory of having been in prison establishes not only who he is when the film begins, but also the difficulties he will face as the film progresses. In addition to clarifying the film's exposition, backstories also give audiences a reason to root for the film's characters to succeed in their quest.

Professions and social backgrounds

The writers of *Liar Liar* knew they had a great high-concept premise on hand when they first came up with the one-line hook: a man has to go an entire day without telling a lie. But the decisions they subsequently made for the lead role were what attracted Jim Carrey to the part, and enabled the film to become one of the biggest hits of 1997. First, they decided that the protagonist should be a divorced man with a spotty commitment to his son, which gave the protagonist an end to work toward. Next, they decided to make him a lawyer. Why? Because lawyers are famous for telling lies. A nuclear physicist or a musician wouldn't have yielded nearly the same amount of comedy because members of those professions aren't notorious for dubious ethics. But a lawyer in the middle of the biggest case of his career who cannot tell a lie was clearly the best, funniest character to undergo that journey.

The first question you should always ask yourself is this: why is this particular character going to benefit from this particular series of circumstances? Matt Damon's underprivileged brainiac in *Good Will*

Hunting wouldn't have been nearly as effective had he been a simply reasonably intelligent but underachieving dropout from a stable, middle-class family; we had to know that he was not only a once-in-a-century genius but also so troubled that without help he would never realize the full extent of his gifts.

Redeeming factors

The good news is that heroes don't always act heroically; in fact, with the exception of action movies, they tend to be quite a good distance from the finish line as far as issues of character are concerned. But neither can they be too morally unbalanced or we won't care enough about them to even bother taking the first step; witness a tale of two Toms – Cruise, that is – as a bitter, self-absorbed jerk in *Rain Man* and a cocky, self-absorbed jerk in *Cocktail*. The former grossed over a hundred million dollars en route to winning an Oscar for Best Picture while the latter celebrated the finer points of dancing while flinging blue drinks into highball glasses. Both films were dramas; both required Cruise's character to do a major overhaul of his priorities by the end of the movie. And yet in *Rain Man*, we understand that Cruise's often unsympathetic actions stem from the sense of lifelong rejection he felt from his father.

In *Cocktail*, there are no such explanations; Cruise is simply a cocky guy whose sole desire is to become a multi-millionaire via some nebulously-defined form of business venture; in the course of his repeated and failed attempts to do so, he gets schooled by an unsympathetic world. And, in examining two films that starred Tom Cruise yet had different results at the box office, we dispel any notion that a star's inherent likeability overrides the choices made by writers when they conceptualize the characters. The bottom line is that audiences will give your protagonist a chance if they feel he is worth redeeming; however, if the protagonist's lousy character qualities seem too much the result of personal choice rather than circumstance, he tends to be written off before their journey has even had a chance to get underway.

Show, don't tell

Just as in real life, it is actions rather than words that provide insight into who a person truly is. Because screenwriters tend to value their words, they are forever battling the temptation to tell the audience all about a character through dialogue rather than show what that character is made of by placing them in situations that constantly test their mettle. Take, for example, a protagonist who has traveled long and far to seek revenge on the man who killed his wife in a drunk-driving accident. Our protagonist finally catches up with the killer only to find that he's a bona fide skid row wino. Naturally, our hero experiences a change of heart and walks away, without having so much as mentioned to the man the nature of his visit. Isn't it clear by our protagonist's actions that though he has been blinded by rage, he is ultimately freed by the new understanding he has? No – or very few – words are necessary; the point is that action is character, and if you can speak volumes about the people in your scripts without their saying a word, you will be well on your way to creating spellbinding, unforgettable characters.

Keeping your protagonist proactive

The adage "give a man a fish and he'll eat for a day, but teach a man to fish and he'll eat for a lifetime" is an apt description of what you want for your protagonist. Simply put, it's better to have your characters actively solve their own problems rather than give them all the tools to do so; not only do we tend to respond better to people who display ingenuity and resourcefulness, but it's also far more exciting and suspenseful for the audience when they truly have no idea how the character is going to get out of the mess they're in.

Case Study

Indiana Jones – A Hero from the Ground Up

If you had to assemble a hero who embodied many of the traits listed above, Indiana Jones would be an excellent place to begin. The writers gave him a simple, immediately understandable backstory and motivation – he was always cheated out of his archaeological discoveries by a smarmy (and, in true villainous fashion, French-accented) rival. Jones' passion for archaeology is cemented immediately by his professional setting; turns out he's not merely a mercenary-minded gold digger, he's a true connoisseur. He's also extremely proactive, as evidenced by the resourcefulness he displays in narrowly avoiding death by booby-trap and rolling boulders in the film's opening sequence. And as if this isn't enough to put the audience squarely in Jones' corner, he's soon pitted against the Nazis – the ultimate villains – in a race to find the fabled, Biblical Ark of the Covenant, an artifact that will bring invincibility to the army that is lucky enough to carry it into battle.

The stakes are high, the obstacles are formidable and Jones ably navigates Herculean task after task with wit and aplomb. But lest the audience believe that Jones will be relegated to the one-dimensionality of heroes past, they give him a not-so-nice quality: an aversion to a serious relationship with the heroine of the movie who will ultimately accompany him on his journey (which, as it turns out, is just the right amount of time to turn Jones' sentiments around). Jones also has a fear of snakes which, although played throughout the film to comic effect, is universal enough to be memorable. And in the end, Jones manages not only to follow his bliss, but to save the free world in the process.

Though the film's success is clearly a product of several other factors – superior direction, impeccable casting, and fresh, tongue-in-cheek homage to the serial heroes of the 1930's and 1940's, just to name a few – it was and is the film's heroic protagonist whose name has made the eponymously-named series synonymous with premier adventure fare.

Antagonists and Supporting Characters

Antagonists

It's often been said that a movie is only as good as its villain; after all, the more formidable the obstacles in your protagonist's way, the more valid her quest and, by extension, the more satisfying her ultimate triumph becomes in the end. As inevitable as it is that the actor who plays a particularly memorable villain will receive much of the credit, it is nonetheless important to recognize that the raw material exists thanks to choices made during the writing stage, long before the actor ever committed to the role. Hannibal Lecter, though unforgettably portrayed by Anthony Hopkins in *The Silence of the Lambs*, was more than a triumph of elocution and mannerisms; indeed, the choice to make him a cultivated, sophisticated – even charming – psychotic cannibal who, on top of it all, had been an extremely successful psychiatrist, was all conceived by the book's author, Thomas Harris, and the writers who adapted the script. Daniel Day-Lewis, in his portrayal of gang leader Bill Cutting, aka "Bill The Butcher" from *Gangs of New York* was deservedly praised for creating as historically accurate an inflection as has ever been seen in the movies, and yet a beautifully-written scene in which he expressed deep sorrow at having killed the only worthy opponent he'd ever known (Leonardo DiCaprio's father) gave an otherwise soulless character some unexpected depth. Just as our heroes can have deep flaws that make us question their character, so can our villains have wonderful qualities that make us question why they turned out to be so awful.

Supporting characters

Supporting characters – by definition anyone who is not the protagonist or on a par with the protagonist (a buddy in a buddy cop movie, the love interest for the romantic lead, etc.) – play a wide variety of roles: understanding wife, wisecracking sidekick, advice-dispensing best friend, etc. While there are more templates and variations on supporting characters than there is room in these pages to discuss them all, there is only one real fact you need to know when populating your script: supporting characters must always be essential to the plot and characters' needs. A person working at a large corporation may, in real life, have numerous superiors, but in a movie it is best to relegate the voice of authority to one character. Ex-girlfriends of a character need only appear if they are going to create conflict in the relationship at the center of the movie. Which is not to say that you should write a large-scale, explosive-filled action film with an eye toward filming it in a vacuum; circumstances like those would certainly call for a number of ancillary speaking roles from time to time. The key is to keep your core group of characters to the bare, essential minimum so that none of them are getting in the way of the story.

Screenwriting Basics: Structure

CHAPTER 4

It's often been said that no one wants to watch a movie about the village of the happy people. Problems – and the pluck and resourcefulness that enable characters to solve them – are part of what allow viewers to suspend their disbelief. The delicate balance of navigating your protagonist through his or her problems in an entertaining fashion is the key to writing a successful screenplay. The root of such a screenplay is based on a three-act structure whose dynamic has often been summed up in the following homily: Act One, get your character up a tree. Act Two, throw rocks at him. Act Three, get him down.

Act I: The Rosetta Stone

If a script can be likened to a tree, then the first act – the initial eighteen to twenty five pages that establishes the film's characters and underlying themes – are the roots. How deeply embedded those roots are in the earth will help determine the fortitude of the tree's bough, branches, and leaves; similarly, most script problems derive from inadequate planning in the first act that leads to confusing or boring events in the ensuing scenes. Thus the first act can be compared to the Rosetta stone of archaeological lore because it must contain nothing less than the essence of the film; every character, theme, and plot device in the best-structured screenplays appears somewhere in those few first pages. The following checklist covers what your first act should include:

The characters

Every first act should make a point to establish the who, what, why, when, and how of your protagonist's life, the lives of those around him, and why these are necessary components for the journey or task that's about to transpire. In the recent hit film *The Incredibles*, we are introduced to Mr. Incredible's entire family: his soon-to-be wife, his best friend FroZone, and eventually his kids. Even the character who will later be revealed as the villain appears in the first act as a semi-deranged prepubescent fan whose help is rejected by Mr. Incredible, thus setting the table for his ultimate revenge. We also know exactly what the protagonist's problem is (relegated to a drab life in the suburbs, he yearns once again for the excitement of his superhero years), how he is going to bring the plot into action (he can't help going out at night and acting like a superhero again) and what the stakes of the movie are (saving the world from the villain's evil plot). All of these characters and their issues are introduced at the beginning of the film, thus laying the groundwork that makes the rest of the story move forward.

The theme of the film

What is this movie about? This question is different from identifying a film's plot; addressing the theme is similar to stating the topic sentence of a five-paragraph essay. Francis Ford Coppola's *The Godfather* is probably among the two or three most beloved films in the history of America cinema, and yet for all its technical virtuosity there is no question that the film's theme – the undertow of family that inevitably and in this case tragically holds sway over even the world's most level-headed characters – is a primary factor in the film's superiority over other more standard Mob fare. Sometimes the theme of a film is stated more directly; witness the 1982 comedy *Trading Places* in which two avaricious banker brothers bet that Eddie Murphy's homeless man can ably fill in for the well-to-do Dan Aykroyd after wondering out loud whether success is the result of nature or nurture. Again, they do so once we have had a chance to meet the characters and establish the ground floor situation for the film that is about to ensue.

The universe in which the film takes place

The universe in which your characters operate should be far more than a mere backdrop; indeed, films ideally take place in a world filled with characters and possibilities that are organic to what the film is about. Home settings, towns, and office situations all need to be fleshed out to fully understand just who the protagonist is. In Mike Judge's underseen-but-much-beloved cult satire *Office Space*, he shows the full, depressing extent of the worlds inhabited by suburban nine-to-fivers: the paper-thin wall apartments, monolithic office parks complete with TGI-Friday's-type lunch establishments (skewered masterfully by Judge as "Tchochke's," where the wait staff must wear requisite amounts of "flair" on their overalls), uncaring bosses, and dehumanizing traffic jams. The comedy flows freely from the situations faced by Judge's characters, but their ultimate triumph lies in their ability to find some smidgen of humanity amidst the oppressive generic nature of their universe.

The inciting incident

The definitive event that happens in the protagonist's life that makes the rest of the movie possible or necessary is known as the "inciting incident." This is the event that signals that the first act has ended (aka the "first act break") and the second act is underway. The first act break – the inciting incident – in *Jerry Maguire* would be when Tom Cruise's character informs his boss, Bob Sugar (played by Jay Mohr) that he is leaving the agency to set out on his own. Prior to this, Maguire had drafted a memo stating what he felt was wrong in the world of sports representation, which led the company for whom he worked to terminate him. This sets Maguire out on his journey: in order to adhere to the lofty values set forth by that memo, Maguire must learn to navigate the tricky, turbulent waters of the sports world – not to mention the real world – on his own. What he ultimately discovers in the course of his journey, and the way he goes from materialistic bottom-liner to empathetic, fully-rounded human being is the basis for the rest of the movie. In *Wall Street*, Charlie Sheen's Bud Fox has gained access to Michael Douglas' rapacious Gordon Gekko, only to find himself floundering to impress Gekko once he's inside Gekko's office. Grasping at straws, he offers up a piece of inside information about his father's airline that impresses Gekko – the film's inciting incident, as from this point on Bud is well on his way to the seductive path of wealth and glamour that will ultimately lead to his demise.

Some other examples of inciting incidents:

- *Elf*: when Will Ferrell's character finds out that he's not an elf, but instead a rather large human.
- *The Texas Chainsaw Massacre*: when Leatherface, the film's killer, claims his first victim and the kids realize that their lives are in danger.
- *Million Dollar Baby*: when Clint Eastwood's character, against his inner leanings, agrees to take on Hilary Swank's character as a trainee.

Act II: The Obstacles

Okay, you've written your inciting incident and your character is officially up a tree. Now, according to the provisions of three-act structure, it's time to throw rocks at him. What does this mean exactly, and how does it make for a more complicated, exciting movie? The second act is the longest part of the script, and is often what makes it or breaks it; if a reader is intrigued by the possibilities established in the first act, only to find that the writer has not fully capitalized on them throughout the course of the second act, there is practically nothing that can be done in the third act to salvage the script. However, if a reader is enjoying a first act considerably, but then finds a treasure trove of plot twists and complications in the second act that makes her flip the pages in anticipation of the third act, the writer can pretty much bank on some good meetings resulting from that script.

Case in point: Dale Launer's terrific script *Ruthless People* began with what seemed like a standard tale of kidnapping and revenge; Judge Reinhold and Helen Slater's characters, frustrated by the greed of Danny DeVito's character who stole their business idea, kidnap his wife (Bette Midler) and threaten to kill her. Two problems – a: they're too nice to kill her, and b: DeVito's character has been trying to kill her all along. As promising as this is as a ground floor scenario, however, it is the triumph of Launer's plotting in the second act that makes the movie truly shine. For DeVito's mistress (Anita Morris) is trying to blackmail DeVito aided by her none-too-bright lover, who videotaped a couple making love rather than what he thought was DeVito killing Midler. When Morris sends the tape to the chief of police, thinking it'll do DeVito in, Launer instead reveals that the chief of police is the one on the tape (cheating on his wife, no less), and in order to keep that tape from surfacing, he'll do anything Morris asks. Meanwhile, DeVito has been telling Reinhold and Slater to kill Midler, while they've been dropping their ransom price in the hopes of getting some money out of him. Through a series of twists and turns that are motivated by that tape, the chief of police moves to arrest DeVito on the grounds of killing Midler. Now, desperate to get Midler back, DeVito tries to negotiate with Reinhold and Slater, who start to drive the price back up after befriending Midler, who it turns out is really just an unhappy woman who, thanks to her imprisonment, loses weight and finally starts to feel good about herself.

The film builds to an unpredictable climax, the surprises never ceasing until the final credits roll. Although *Ruthless People* has a Byzantine cast of characters, its plotting – specifically, its second act – is a model to which aspiring writers should turn to as a paradigm of great structure.

In the absence of a great farcical structure like *Ruthless People*, what kinds of devices should you turn to in order to ratchet up the jeopardy or drama faced by your protagonist? Here are a few tips:

1. **A ticking clock:** Give your character a finite amount of time in which she has to complete the task at hand. This raises the stakes for the protagonist

– and by extension, the excitement for the audience. To return once again to *The Silence of the Lambs*, Jodie Foster's FBI agent plays a game of mental chess with the incarcerated Hannibal Lecter, but the clock is ticking: if she cannot get Lecter to reveal the necessary information, a young girl will be slaughtered by a vicious serial killer. To drive this point home, director Jonathan Demme not only cuts away to the serial killer (whose lair is surely one the creepiest in film history) but also informs us of the killer's plan, which involves starving some weight off the girl so he can skin her. More important than the shock value conveyed by this gruesome detail is its structural importance: we have been put on notice that unless Foster's character is successful in a certain amount of time, the girl will die.

Not all ticking clocks are as dire as the example offered by *Silence of the Lambs*, however. Comedies also make good use of the jeopardy that time can permit for, as evidenced by the delightful *Bill and Ted's Excellent Adventure* in which time – literally – is of the essence. If Bill and Ted do not use their time machine to collect enough historical figures and bring them back to San Dimas by 2:30 p.m. the next day, they will fail their report (which will lead to an improbable, but well-explained cataclysm of events that will prevent the future from being as glorious as it is). The interesting conceit in *Bill and Ted's* is that despite their ability to use their time machine to bend time as they see fit, Bill and Ted cannot manipulate time in the present; thus, as George Carlin's character explains while holding up his watch, "the clock is always ticking in the present and you've got to be back by 2:30."

2. **Internal and external conflict:** You've established the who, what, why, where, and how of the protagonist in the first act; now it's time to put the ancient Greeks' adage "drama is conflict" to the test. Conflict, in the dramatic sense, means anything that prevents the character from getting what he wants and is usually divided into two categories: external and internal. An antagonist certainly qualifies as a form of external conflict, as he is doing everything in his power to stand in the protagonist's way. An especially Herculean task, such as the one faced by Adam Sandler's character, who has to woo a short-term amnesiac every single day in *50 First Dates*, constitutes external conflict, as the situation continuously gets in the way of Sandler's goal to marry Drew Barrymore.

   Internal conflict also works to keep the protagonist from realizing his goal, only unlike the outside forces that conspire to bring him down, internal conflict aims to trip up the protagonist from within. In Paul Attanasio's magnificent screenplay for *Quiz Show*, a film about the quiz show cheating scandals of the 1950s (but, like all great films, one that is about much more than its baseline premise), Ralph Fiennes' Charles Van Doren is aware that, in being given the answers to the show's questions, he is being asked to do something scandalous. But he is tempted, not only by the lure of television fame, but by the idea that perhaps being packaged as a national genius might address his feelings of inferiority in the wake of his father's formidable intellectual legacy. Thus the conflict, which as with many internal conflicts, is often presented in the form of a choice: does Van Doren do the exciting thing or does he do the right thing? Unfortunately for Van Doren (but fortunately for film aficionados for whom *Quiz Show* ranks as one of the truly great American screenplays), he chooses the latter.

3. **Subplots:** A subplot is a device that will help flesh out your story and keep you from running out of gas in the middle of what can at times feel like a Saharan second act. Subplots, which are also known as "B" stories (or "C" or "D," depending on how many of them there are), are stories that relate to either the protagonist's journey or the theme of the movie.

   Say, for example, you are writing a film about the investigation of a possible serial killer; the subplot could involve the introduction of another possible suspect (a device known as a "red herring," introduced to keep the audience from guessing the ending). If you are writing a romantic comedy, the subplot could either involve another potential suitor for the female protagonist or another separate romance involving her best friend. If you are writing a sports movie about a coach who turns an underachieving team into a bunch of winners, the subplot(s) would involve the lives of the players off the court – a girlfriend with an unwanted pregnancy, a player who is facing the prospect of expulsion after failing his classes, etc. (both of which were employed in the recent hit film *Coach Carter*). If you are writing an ensemble piece on the order of *Diner* or *Stand By Me*, each of the characters will have a story which will amount to several subplots, yet there will almost always be a protagonist whose journey will define those of the people around him as well.

4. **Setpieces, aka trailer moments:** If you ever read or listen to reports about the movie business, you've probably heard the phrase "trailer moment" bandied about. A trailer moment, also known as a "setpiece," is a sequence told mostly in images that is traditionally very action-heavy and is geared either to bring the audience to its knees with laughter or to the edge of its collective seat with excitement (and is referred to as a trailer moment due to its inevitable inclusion in the film's upcoming trailer, which will entice viewers into wanting to see the film).

With the exception of traditional drama, virtually every genre film will have a preponderance of setpieces in the second act (and, as we will discuss later, the third act, which sometimes can resemble one long setpiece). If you are writing a comedy, it is crucial to get your protagonist into a situation where, to invoke a cliché, hilarity ensues. Say, for example, your protagonist is an undercover detective who has been forced to wear a dress to infiltrate a women's sorority, where a bunch of killings are taking place. And yet the very night he's supposed to be at the sorority house for initiation, his fiancée (who must be kept in the dark about his actions for security purposes) invites him to dinner with her wealthy parents, who are only in town for the night. A comic setpiece in which the detective would have to run back and forth from sorority initiation to dinner with his fiancee's parents, requiring not only quick changes but several stammering explanations along the way. If you are writing a thriller, you would most likely have several cat-and-mouse chase scenes, or stalking sequences, in which we would see a shadowy suspect narrowly escape apprehension by the protagonist, or the protagonist narrowly avoid being killed by the villain. As stated earlier, "action is character," because film is a visual medium (which will be addressed further when we discuss the "show, don't tell" aspects of screenwriting). You must always construct situations that will force your characters into action, which will not only excite the audience but will better define your characters as well.

The second plot point

The second act ends on a plot point that puts the protagonist in position for the film's climax. By now all the obstacles have been eliminated, leaving the protagonist poised for a battle with the villain, or with one last external set of circumstances that lie before him. In *The Graduate*, the second plot point occurs when Benjamin realizes that Elaine is getting married, thus forcing him to embark on one last frenetic journey to halt the wedding. In *Seven*, the second plot point occurs when the serial killer turns himself in, thus setting the stage for the final two deadly sins to play out in an unforgettable climax. Romantic comedies tend to have the girl find out something about the guy – usually a misunderstanding that's no longer applicable, like he's just been in it for the money – that leads her to break up with him (witness 2005's runaway hit *Hitch*). The point is that no matter the genre, something important happens that brings the protagonist's journey through the second act to its conclusion, and now it's time to resolve his struggle once and for all.

Act III: Climax and Resolution

The movie's last plot point has been revealed, setting the final battle or conflict in place-it's time to go out with a bang. What should your third act entail? If you're writing a thriller, your hero is going to take on the villain in one last confrontation. If you've been working on a romantic comedy, the hero understands the error of his ways that led to the breakup, and must now convince the girl of his worthiness. A few things to keep in mind when constructing your third act:

- **Keep your protagonist active:** Nothing frustrates readers (and audiences) more than a protagonist who has heroically prevailed against a series of Herculean tasks, only to become a passive, unresourceful lug in the third act. A man who has lost the woman with whom he has worked so hard to fall in love (again, witness *Hitch*) can't win her back simply by asking her sister to talk to the woman for him. Likewise, a detective who has uncovered clue after clue and has pieced together what otherwise seems like an unsolvable case wouldn't then crack it based on an anonymous tip that lands miraculously in her lap. Your hero has proven himself worthy and has dodged all the rocks you've thrown his way; now it's up to you to let him find his own way down the tree.

- **When at all possible, tie your theme to the story:** If the theme of your movie is "power corrupts" and the protagonist is someone whose world collapses due to his pursuit of power, then he must challenge that very power structure (Oliver Stone's underrated but still-potent *Wall Street* comes to mind; Charlie Sheen's character must now summon up all his strength – his true power – in order to save his father's airline and foil Gekko, the man whose world he has so strived to become part of). You won't always be able to directly address your theme; certain genres are more plot-driven, thus the confluence of events that leads into the third act will be a sufficient platform on which to end your movie.

- **Twists:** On that note, should you use a twist ending? The answer is yes, if your film offers you the opportunity. If you are writing a drama about a woman running a poor homestead in a rural Southern community at the turn of the century, then it's pretty safe to assume that a shocking twist (It was only a dream after all! She's really a man!) would be too strange for the audience to absorb. On the other hand, if you're writing a thriller, the audience is going to expect a twist... only it can't be the one they expected. A twist is a terrific way to send your movie out with a bang, but only if executed properly, as in the following case study.

Tips on Screenplay Structure

1. **Act breakdown:** Now that you have learned the basic three-act structure, you should know roughly where these acts come with relation to your page count. Act One should run roughly 18-25 pages; Act Two should be anywhere from 55-65 pages; Act Three should range from 15-20 pages, for a script totaling between 100 and 120 pages.

2. **The difference between a story and a plot:** A story is a series of events that happen one after the other. A plot is a series of events that happen one because of the other. The best film plots are comprised of scenes that expound on the scene prior and spill effortlessly into the scene ensuing. Think of it as a quilt, in which each patch of fabric is a scene that, if removed, would unravel the entire thing.

3. **Four quarters, or mid-point pivots:** Around halfway through the film, characters often hit "fail-safe" points where they are faced with a choice to continue on or quit. Their insistence to forge ahead in their quest is what is commonly known as a mid-point pivot because it occurs at the mid-point of a movie and involves a character making a decision that, prior to his or her journey, would have been unthinkable. At the mid-point of the recent hit film *The Pacifier*, Vin Diesel's character goes from a kid-hating grump to a guy who learns to love the kids he is in charge of guarding, as exemplified in the scene where he dances for a little kid who refers to him as *Daddy*. However, there is a school of thought that considers this pivot a legitimate act break (thus breaking the film into four quarters, rather than three acts). If this helps structure the film better in your head and make the second act feel a bit less formidable, then by all means employ this model.

Case Study

Fight Club and _The Sixth Sense_ – A Tale of Two Twists

The films *Fight Club* and *The Sixth Sense* were both released in 1999. Both featured major stars, although while *Fight Club* was touted as a can't-miss hit, *The Sixth Sense* so scared its parent studio, Disney, that they sold off virtually all the film's rights in order to hedge their bets.

Both films featured major plot twists that virtually no viewer claimed to have seen coming (save for fans of Chuck Palahniuk's book who, of course, were not surprised). And yet, in a strange twist of its own, *Fight Club* ended up losing money at the box office while *The Sixth Sense* became one of the highest grossing films of all time.

So what happened? *Fight Club* told the story of two men who, distressed by America's emasculating consumerist culture, create a bare-knuckles fight-club. One of the men is unnamed (save for some comic monikers he uses at the various self-help groups he frequents), but the other, far more unbalanced of the two, is named Tyler Durden. The men, now having had a primal urge awakened within them, graduate to increasingly anarchic and outrageous deeds, climaxing in a scheme to destroy all of the country's credit unions. However, just as we are about to lurch into the third act in which the ultimate plan is revealed, there is a plot twist (don't read on if you haven't seen the movie and want to be surprised) – our unnamed protagonist and Tyler Durden are one and the same.

Fight Club enjoys legions of loyal fans and has developed something of a cult following in the years since its release. It is an interesting, provocative piece of work, a film the viewer doesn't shake so easily after having viewed it. And yet to understand why it underperformed at the box office, one need look no further than the film's twist ending. Was it really necessary to take a film that was on the verge of making a truly disturbing point about the mind and soul-numbing nature of consumerism and turn it instead into a man's journey into schizophrenia? The book enjoyed a small measure of success, but movies – especially ones that cost as much as *Fight Club* did – must cross over into a much larger segment of the population, and *Fight Club* unfortunately involved too unwieldy a plot for audiences to wrap themselves around. Even the star power of Brad Pitt and Edward Norton, combined with a moody atmosphere as realized by David Fincher (who'd also directed the phenomenally successful *Seven* and *Alien 3*) couldn't save it from disappointing the producers and studio executives who'd had such high hopes for it.

The Sixth Sense, on the other hand, concerned the executives at Disney to no end. No one could figure out how to sell it – was it a supernatural thriller with touches of horror, or a psychological thriller with a dreamy, bittersweet ending? Bruce Willis, the film's star, had enjoyed a formidable career as an action star, but how would audiences react to a film that portrayed him as a sensitive child psychologist? The parties involved knew the film had a killer twist ending, but would it be coming two hours into a movie that had audiences snoozing in their seats at the slowly-paced, mutedly spiritual film? Concerned, they split the costs with an equity partner which would cover them in case the film flopped.

The Sixth Sense, buoyed by almost uniformly positive reviews, opened with over thirty-five million dollars. Then something truly extraordinary happened. Rather than drop off thirty or forty, or even fifty percent, as most films do in their second weekend, *The Sixth Sense* dropped off zero. Word of mouth was so strong that people who otherwise wouldn't have seen the film flocked to see it. Why? The word was that the film had the most unpredictable twist anyone had ever seen. But not just an unpredictable one, as it turned out. One that made complete sense, that put the whole movie in perspective. Bruce Willis' character, Malcolm, prevails on Cole, the character played by Haley Joel Osment, to tell him why he's so troubled. "I see dead people," the kid tells him in one of the film's most famous lines. But this has already happened well after Malcolm has been shot and has emerged seemingly physically unscathed from the incident, so that we as the audience don't put two and two together. The rest of the film details how Malcolm helps Cole, all the while trying to figure out why his own wife has been so distant toward him. Not until the very end do we learn the truth.

Is it airtight? Not really; Cole knows the people he sees are dead, so he could easily share this information with Malcolm when Malcolm wonders about the distance between him and his wife. However the structural sleight of hand that the film's writer/director, M. Night Shyamalan employs sets up the twist so ingeniously that it takes a second or third viewing of the film to truly understand what has been going on all along. The twist, consequently, doesn't feel tacked-on or perfunctory; it shocks the tears out of us, which is why the film made such a profound impact on just about everyone who saw it.

Case Study

Back to the Future

Robert Zemeckis and Robert Gale's script for the 1985 film *Back To The Future* was borne of the universal desire that everyone has to go back in time and see what their parents were like as teenagers. With this premise as their launch point, they constructed a comic science-fiction fantasy that ultimately became the first film in a highly successful (if slightly uneven) trilogy. And yet for all the critical and commercial acclaim heaped on *Back To The Future*, its greatest enduring legacy very well might be a flawless character and structural model that offers a bounty of lessons for screenwriters everywhere.

The opening shot of the movie tells the viewer a great deal about where the film is headed, and what it is about. As we pan down a crazy invention, we see clock after clock, as well as a few tidbits of background information that give us expositional clues we will need to know later: a clipping detailing the destruction of the Brown mansion as well as a news report about a theft of plutonium. Time is of the essence, the camera seems to be telling us, a motif that will factor into the movie in more ways than one.

The first act then goes on to introduce the film's characters. Marty McFly is a good-looking teenager who is friends with a crackpot inventor named Doc Brown (whose laboratory is featured in the film's opening shot). As he's accosted by his principal, he's told that his band shouldn't even bother trying out for the school dance because no McFly has ever amounted to anything in the history of Hill Valley. "Yeah?" responds Marty. "Well history's gonna change." Here, Marty has summed up the film's theme, or topic sentence – not only can history change, but it'll happen through a defiant, can-do spirit that is, as we'll soon find out, direly lacking in the modern-day McFlys.

But Marty's band doesn't pass the audition, and Marty is consumed by doubt – maybe he isn't any good, he muses out loud. Then he realizes he sounds just like his father. Marty and his girlfriend are about to kiss when they're interrupted by a woman who urges them to restore the town's clock tower, which was hit by lightning thirty years prior. She hands Marty and his girlfriend a flyer, the back of which Marty's girlfriend uses to write down the number where she'll be before scooting off; without the audience knowing it, the writers have introduced a key piece of information – namely, the clock tower and the precise time and date it was hit by lightning.

We are then introduced to Marty's family at home, but more importantly we meet the film's villain, Biff, who is introduced blaming George McFly for a blind spot in the car that Biff claims led to him having an accident. We discover that George McFly is a coward who cannot stand up to Biff (he even does Biff's reports for him) and that George's wife, Lorraine, is a lush who fell in love with George because Lorraine's father accidentally hit George with his car years ago, causing a Nightingale effect (nurses falling in love with their patients) when Lorraine nursed George back to health. Additionally, we find out that George and Lorraine kissed for the first time at the Enchantment Under The Sea Dance, and that it was then that Lorraine knew she was destined to spend the rest of her life with George.

This is all a great deal of set-up, to be sure, but not only is it delivered in entertaining fashion, it will soon prove to be the basis for the rest of the film. It's excellent character work as well; we have sympathy for Marty, as he's something of an underdog, as well as for his parents who seem decent but beaten-down by their inability to stand up to and rise above the challenges that life offers up.

Marty meets Doc Brown later that night, only to find out that Doc has stolen the aforementioned stash of plutonium from a group of Libyan nationalists who wanted him to build them a nuclear bomb. Doc instead used the plutonium to create a time machine... out of a DeLorean sports car, one of the film's many comic flourishes. Doc demonstrates how the time machine works, making a point to type in the date in the past when he first "discovered" time travel. A struggle ensues between Doc and the Libyans, at which point Doc is shot. Marty hops in the time machine, guns the engine, and is transported back to the year Doc entered (which, we will soon find out, coincides with the period when George met Lorraine). This is the end of the first act – the inciting incident that makes the film's events (Marty's trip into the past) possible – and the obstacles that are about to ensue are as memorable as any in recent film history.

Marty then finds out that not only is he stranded in 1955 without any plutonium left to get him back to the present day, he's also managed to interfere with his parents' introduction, which leads to one very unforeseen, unwelcome twist – apparently his own mother "has the hots" for him. As if this isn't bad enough, Marty realizes (through a family photo) that as the result of his having interfered with his parents' introduction, he and his brother and sister are being erased from existence. He must get George and Lorraine together... only there are yet further obstacles to contend with. For George is not only a teenaged version of the coward we met as an adult, he's completely unaware of and inept with girls. Marty takes him under his wing and tries to get him to ask Lorraine out, but herein lies another obstacle. Namely Biff, whose teenaged self is alive and well in 1955, up to the same bullying tactics vis-à-vis George, and is interested in Lorraine to boot. So now not only does Marty have to refocus his mother's affections from him to George, he must fend off Biff while doing it-all before the Enchantment Under The Sea Dance, which is the same night the bolt of lightning will strike the clock tower (which Doc Brown has figured out a way to rig up to the time machine, thus sending Marty back to the future). Thus Zemeckis and Gale have established not one, but two ticking clocks (the lightning hitting the clock tower, the Enchantment Under The Sea Dance) that drive the second act's urgency. What adds to the film's enjoyment, in addition to the numerous setpieces (the chase scene around the town square with Marty on a makeshift skateboard that culminates in Biff hitting a manure truck is especially fun) and inside jokes ("Who's President of the U.S. in 1985?" "Ronald Reagan." "Ronald Reagan? The actor???") is the underlying notion that we truly do not know how Marty will overcome all the hurdles Zemeckis and Gale have placed in his path; in addition to foiling Biff while getting his parents together, there is also the nagging question of how Marty will help save Doc from getting shot by the Libyans in the present day. Every event in the second act necessitates the scenes that ensue; there is not a moment of flab anywhere in the story.

Not only does Marty succeed in engineering a scheme for George to unite with Lorraine, it goes better than his wildest dreams. George, through a confluence of events (which, it turns out, end up forcing him to be resourceful and brave on his own and not rely on the plan that Marty had scripted for him) winds up knocking Biff out cold, then Marty has enough time not only to make it to the DeLorean, but to play guitar while George and Lorraine finally enjoy their first kiss. Marty tries to slip a note into Doc's pocket, warning him of the fate that will befall him in the future, but Doc pays it no heed – he warns against the dangers of knowing your future, and rips the note into pieces. We are treated to an extraordinary setpiece where Marty is sent back to the future by the skin of his teeth – having set the car's clock ten minutes earlier so that he'll be able to warn Doc in the future – only to have the car fail on him once he's safely back in 1985. Zemeckis and Gale have finished their second act – the point at which the protagonist, Marty, has overcome all the obstacles in his way – and are ready for one final showdown.

Which comes in the form of Marty's rushing back to the site of Doc's original experiment... just in time to see Doc get shot by the Libyans. Marty starts to cry; his best efforts weren't good enough. But wait! Doc's eyes flutter and he rips open his suit jacket to reveal a bulletproof vest. Doc then pulls Marty's taped-together letter out his pocket, telling Marty that his curiosity got the better of him.

And then the movie's final coda kicks in. For everything Zemeckis and Gale have set up now fully pays off, as Marty wakes up in his bed only to find that his family has undergone a transformation. Gone is the Burger King uniform his brother was sporting; now he's dressed in a three-piece suit. His chubby, unpopular sister is still chubby, only now she's juggling boyfriends with ease. And Marty's mother and father stroll in, dressed in tennis casual attire, flush with confidence and success, as Biff (who now has been relegated to detailing the McFlys' cars) enters excitedly, holding a box of George's new books (back in 1955 it was revealed that George wanted to be a science-fiction writer, only he lacked the confidence). History, per Marty's prediction, has changed; Zemeckis and Gale tell an exciting story that is made all the more so due to their strict adherence to the rules of three-act structure.

Case Study

Working Girl

The 1987 Kevin Wade-scripted comedy *Working Girl*, is another example of three-act structure executed to perfection. Melanie Griffith's character, Tess McGill, is a working-class girl from Staten Island who is a secretary on Wall Street. Tess is established as a plucky, smart young woman who, due to class barriers, has been denied access to the higher echelons of Wall Street despite her hard work and resourcefulness. She is humiliated by the male power structure (even getting sent on what she believes is a job interview, only to realize that she is being asked to function as an escort). Tess, however, is no pushover; she exacts her revenge on her tormentors and is ultimately transferred to the desk of Sigourney Weaver's Katherine Parker, a well-educated upper-crust young woman (two months younger than Tess, as Katherine proudly points out) who appears to be the epitome of everything Tess wants out of life. Katherine presents herself as a mentor and Tess goes along, even excitedly telling her uninterested lug of a boyfriend, played by Alec Baldwin, all about Katherine. Thus is the first act constructed; we are shown the inequality of the world in which Tess lives, as well as the unyielding obstacles that stubbornly lie in her way.

The first act ends when Katherine asks Tess to housesit for her while she is away, skiing in Germany. Katherine then injures herself, requiring her to remain in Germany for a little while longer. At which point Tess discovers that the idea she'd brought Katherine – a purchase of radio stations for a company named Trask – has been stolen by Katherine with the intent of passing it off as her own. That night, Tess returns home to find her boyfriend having sex with another woman. Tess gets onto the Staten Island Ferry, her world in tatters.

So let's review what has happened to Tess in the first twenty or so minutes of the movie: she has essentially been told that the world of which she wants to be a part is closed to her, and that the one woman who might have helped make that possible is a snake and a liar. To boot, her boyfriend is unfaithful. Left with seemingly few options, Tess makes a radical decision: she will impersonate an investment banker and put the deal that she proposed to Katherine together herself.

Now let's stop and think for a moment. If someone you knew told you that they had decided to pretend that they were someone they weren't at work and decided to bring other investment bankers in on the ruse (as Tess soon does with Harrison Ford's character, Jack), what would be your response? Once you were through being horrified, you'd probably get their boss on the phone – if not the police. The last thing you would do is find their antics charming... and yet that is exactly the reaction the writer of *Working Girl* not only asks, but expects of you. Why? Because Tess has been backed into a corner, and the writer has made it abundantly clear that only through desperate measures will her goals (of which she is more than deserving) be met. Tess has established herself as a sympathetic character, but more importantly her nemesis has warranted Tess' response, thus further establishing our approval of Tess' actions.

Once Tess decides to pass herself off as an investment banker, she contacts Jack, who Katherine had specified as the banker to whom she wanted to bring the deal. To increase the stakes, we find out that Jack is a banker whose career has taken a turn for the worse; he needs this deal almost as badly as Tess does. But first we are treated to a hilarious introduction, where Tess winds up getting drunk and passing out on Jack prior to realizing who he is. Then, once Tess and Jack are formally introduced, they set out to put their deal together. And it is at this point in the film where Tess' true gifts become apparent. She doesn't have weeks to wait for a meeting with Trask, so with Jack at her side she crashes Trask's daughter's wedding and introduces her idea to Trask while dancing with him. Then she and Jack pitch the idea to Trask's people, who are initially cool to the idea until Tess and Jack brainstorm some on-the-spot logic that the old man approves (through another hilarious scene in which Trask is portrayed as an invisible, yet omnipresent deity who, in the words of his snide underling, "hears everything").

Now that the deal looks like it will happen, Jack and Tess are free to consummate the passion that has been brewing between them... only Tess now finds out that Jack is the lover to whom Katherine has made reference... and Katherine is due to return any moment (as good a ticking time clock device as any in recent cinema). All the while Tess' best friend Cynthia (played with aplomb by Joan Cusack), warns her that "sometimes I like to dance around my apartment in my underwear. Doesn't make me Madonna. Never will." But Tess is far too enamored of her new life to pay heed; having come so close to what she has always wanted (and rightly deserved), she'll be damned if she's going to take back her cheating boyfriend and subservient position as a demeaned secretary.

And yet shortly thereafter, the entire ruse comes crashing down. The second act ends with Katherine coming home and finding Tess's appointment book in her house, which lists all the details of the deal with Trask. Katherine marches into the meeting and reveals that Tess is, in fact, her secretary, but that she is now there to take full credit and move the deal forward. Tess is shamed in front of not only everyone she has worked so hard to impress, but in front of Jack as well. The movie would have us believe that Tess risked everything and cleared every hurdle and obstacle that stood in her way, only to wind up with nothing.

But since this is a romantic comedy, there is destined to be a third act that will yield a happy ending. Tess has traversed the obstacles, the latest of which seems to be an impasse that will wipe out all of her good work. And yet while reading the gossip pages of the Daily News (which we find out she does in order to get ideas), she comes across an item that could possibly prove fatal to the deal that she has helped put together. She bumps into Jack and the deal team in the lobby of her building after having cleaned out her desk and mentions this to them. Jack, believing her, climbs into the elevator with Tess (along with Trask, who is sufficiently persuaded as well), and Tess explains the genesis of the Trask deal. Trask, upon exiting the elevator, confronts Katherine who can't supply the same information that Tess has given, and Katherine is summarily dismissed. Tess winds up with a job in Trask's empire, moves in with Jack, and all ends well.

A seemingly simple story, *Working Girl* is nonetheless as good a paradigm of screenwriting rules as any. Fueled by the engine of mistaken identity – always a great plot device – its story is wonderfully stakes-driven; Tess is fighting not only for a high-profile deal, but for the best shot at success she will probably ever see in this life. The events happen one because of the other, and all due to the actions of a protagonist who leaves nothing to chance and, who in the end, gets the love of her life as well.

Screenwriting Basics: Dialogue and Scene

CHAPTER 5

It is often said that a good writer "has an ear for dialogue." Indeed, of all the components of screenwriting, dialogue is perhaps the one that is toughest to teach and relies the most upon natural gifts that you either do or do not have. That said, there are tips to writing better dialogue that can be learned, and the scenes constructed by the interactions between characters must be propelled by dynamics that will make your script a much more powerful read in the end. Two people walking and talking is never as interesting as one person trying to extract information from another – scenes must have a point, and to that end your characters' dialogue (or lack thereof) must realize that.

Dialogue

Some pointers you want to keep in mind whenever you're writing dialogue:

1. Dialogue versus conversation: One of the most important lessons you will ever learn as a screenwriter – especially when it comes time to self-edit – is what the difference is between conversation and dialogue. Simply put, dialogue is conversation with a point, with subtext. Dialogue must either move the characters or the plot forward, and in the best, most economically-written screenplays, you won't find so much as a wasted syllable. Take, for example, the following exchange:

BOB
Hey there, Stan.

STAN
Hey there, Bob.

BOB
What's going on?

STAN
Oh, nothing. How about you?

BOB
Nothing. Are you going over to Thelma's later?

STAN

Yeah.

This might be a perfectly viable conversation that two people could have in real life, but the fact is that you just filled up nearly half of a page while essentially informing us nothing about either Bob or Stan, or about what their objectives are vis-à-vis the plot. Now, take for example, the following patch of dialogue:

BOB

Saw you over at Thelma's the other night

STAN

So?

BOB

So I thought things were over between you two.

Now, in three simple lines, Bob has elicited an important piece of information from Stan: that he was at Thelma's the other night. Stan, in his response, implies defensiveness, which sparks the reader's curiosity. Which is then answered, somewhat, by Bob's informing us that there was a history between Stan and Thelma that is clearly being revisited.

Subtext is the art of implication, of alluding to more than the characters are outright saying. For example, let's say a character said something on the order of this:

MAXINE

Fred told me he loved me.

(beat)

He told me a lot of things.

We could reasonably intuit that Maxine is a character who has been burned by a man named Fred; she doesn't outright say "I've been burned by a man named Fred," but this is the subtext of what she is saying in this line of dialogue.

2. Exposition, and how to avoid it: One of the most difficult challenges you will face in the course of writing a screenplay is how to get relevant information across without it being needlessly expository (which is inevitably boring). Take, for example, the following sample:

SAM

Better be back before five o'clock, at which point Jay, the villain who's been after us for two years, will be back to blow our heads off.

It's not that the audience doesn't need to know all this information, it's that the manner in which it is delivered is so clumsily direct (or "on the nose," in screenwriting parlance) that it comes off as laughable. Now take the same information, only written like this:

SAM

Jay's gonna be back at five o'clock. Which means you'd better be back by four thirty, unless you want two years of ducking and dodging the man to go down the drain.

The content of this dialogue hasn't changed-but the manner in which that content is delivered makes all the difference.

3. Show, don't tell: Film is a visual medium. The prevailing mantra in your head as a screenwriter should be "show, don't tell." When you watch a movie, it's always a good idea to note just how little dialogue actually takes place. Keep in mind that, when you are watching a movie, it is always far more exciting to see characters acting on their decisions rather than pontificating on them. Which means that, whenever possible, you should be trying to avoid needless dialogue and focus instead on visuals that will help tell your story. For example, take the following passage:

MARK

What's that over there?

KIM

Where?

MARK

There, by the dock. That shadowy figure.

KIM

Should we go over and investigate?

Clearly you need to establish the presence of something nefarious that must be addressed within the framework of the scene. But here might be a more economical, filmic way to do so:

> Mark and Kim are making their way over to the dock when all of a sudden Mark STOPS walking.
>
> KIM
>
> What?
>
> Mark, his face going white, just points over to the dock, where we see…
>
> A SHADOWY FIGURE
>
> standing there, watching them.
>
> A beat. Then, summoning up all his courage, Mark gestures for Kim to follow him.

In the above example, one word of dialogue was all that was necessary. The rest of the information was conveyed through visuals, which, if accompanied by a heart-palpitating score and the right cinematography, will bring a viewer to the edge of his or her seat.

4. The button: A scene's "button" – the term used for ending, or "buttoning" up a scene – should be a punchy moment that either reflects a terrific line delivered by one of the characters or a moment of suspense that bridges effortlessly into the next scene. One thing you definitely don't want to do is write past the button. For example, a scene's natural button might run something like this:

> RICHARD
>
> That kind of talk is exactly what I'm talking about.

Whereas an example of writing past the button would sound something like this:

> RICHARD
>
> That kind of talk is exactly what I'm talking about.
>
> LAURA
>
> Okay. Bye.

RICHARD

Bye.

On the other hand, some narration followed by a camera shot might work perfectly fine. For example:

RICHARD

That kind of talk is exactly what I'm talking about.

As Laura takes this in…

You would end the scene there, at Laura's reaction. The point is to conclude the scene as snappily as possible, giving the reader no chance to pause or put the script down.

5. Rileys: Your dialogue, when written on the page, should ideally be self-explanatory; you shouldn't have to explain in any way the spirit in which, the line is intended to be delivered. Parentheticals under the characters' names that precede the dialogue they are about to speak are known in the industry as "rileys." As in:

SAMANTHA

(wryly)

You gonna wear a hat with that?

Since the first thing actors tend to do when they receive a script is cross out such suggestions, you might as well dispense with them entirely. On the other hand, there are instances when a quick note of clarification, or emphasis, isn't such a bad idea. Especially if it can be done with a touch of flair. As in:

SAMANTHA

(you must be joking)

You gonna wear a hat with that?

If the parenthetical can reveal a dash of subtext and convey what the character is thinking in concrete terms while they're delivering the line, then the suggestion tends to be far more welcome. Just as in writing narrative, it is important to remember that the script will be read before it will ever be filmed; the more you can do to make it an entertaining read, the more likely it is that a reader will respond to it.

6. Editing and triage: Most writers aren't particularly good at self-editing; naturally, it is one's wont to believe that everything one has written is perfect and should remain as is. And yet the adage "writing is rewriting" sums up the process in a nutshell. Contrary to the conventional wisdom behind taking multiple choice exams, your first instinct is rarely the right choice; you must continue exploring other dialogue options or, in keeping with the rule of "show, don't tell," no dialogue options. Look at each scene and brutally examine every line, asking yourself: is it necessary? Am I conveying something important about my characters, or moving the plot forward? Could it be shorter or written in a voice more consistent with that of the character thus far? Difficult though it may be to be completely objective about your dialogue, you owe it not only to yourself but to your characters as well.

Scene

Achieving the perfect flow of a scene is, after dialogue, probably the most difficult aspect of screenwriting to teach. One thing to keep in mind is that there is no such thing as a "perfect scene," there are only perfect scenes for any particular script and the particular needs of that script's characters. That said, it is always worth analyzing a few scenes from recent movies to determine precisely what makes them so great, and the lessons they hold for all screenwriters, regardless of their professional expertise. The following is a list of scenes that exemplify some of the best aspects of screenwriting:

1. *Goodfellas* – Funny? How?: Joe Pesci's introduction in Martin Scorsese's 1990 film *Goodfellas* ranks as among the most quoted scenes in movie history. Rightfully so, as Pesci's "what the fuck makes me so fuckin' funny?" was that all-too-elusive perfect moment in screenwriting – namely a defining refrain that sums up the essence of a character. But what makes the scene so extraordinary from a screenwriting perspective is that it manages to elicit several different responses from the viewer in the course of the four-plus minutes that elapse.

When we first meet Tommy D (Pesci), he is regaling his friends with an anecdote. He is in mid-stream; we don't necessarily know exactly what the story is about, but we see the reverential silence afforded Tommy as he tells a story (for reasons that go beyond Tommy's considerable gifts as a raconteur, as we will soon find out). Tommy's story eventually winds down to his taking a tough guy stance and refusing to tell a policeman anything except "go fuck your mother." The punchline – not an especially funny one save for Pesci's tremendous delivery, but entirely appropriate given the wit level (or lack thereof) in this universe – is that, upon coming to, Pesci asks the cop, "You still here? I thought I told you to go fuck your mother." The table explodes in laughter and so do we; Tommy strikes us not only as a funny, entertaining guy but as a loyal member of the crew as well.

And then Henry (played by Ray Liotta) makes the mistake of telling Tommy that he's funny. Tommy's face registers surprise – funny? "How?" he asks. "You know, the way you tell the story. It's funny." But Tommy continues to register his surprise that Henry would feel this way, and in no time Tommy's surprise turns to anger that Henry would purport to view him as "some kind of clown." The rage consumes Tommy as he pivots from good-time Charlie to rage-a-holic who seems to be about a second away from a violent outburst, and the viewer, sensing this, feels every bit as uncomfortable as Henry. There is a long pause, then Henry tells Tommy to "get the fuck out of here," and Tommy cracks up. "I don't know about you, Henry," he says. "You might not hold up under questioning." Not only does Tommy garner a good laugh at Henry's expense, he also foreshadows what will, in the end, be the downfall of this particular sect of the Mob – namely, Henry's turning state's evidence against them.

This would have been a perfectly appropriate place to end the scene, save for one thing. Tommy is not a "goodfella" – a fact that will soon be played out in gory detail – thus the scene cannot end on an indication that it's all fun and games with him. So the relief that the viewer experiences (the third such emotional spike the scene evokes) is short-lived as the restaurant's owner comes over to settle the bill. Tommy tells the guy to put it on his tab, which the restaurant owner informs him is five thousand dollars; he'd like it settled. Tommy takes issue with this and accuses the owner of embarrassing him in front of his friends. And before the viewer can react, Tommy picks up a bottle and smashes it against the owner's head. The owner runs off in agony as the mobsters all laugh, and once again the viewer is properly horrified. And the scene, appropriately enough, buttons up on Tommy's line: "Wanna hear something really funny? Just last week this prick asked me to baptize his kid." We exit the scene shaking our heads at the ping-ponging of laughter and shock to which our emotions have been subjected.

2. *Pulp Fiction* – Mrs. Mia Wallace O.D.'s: When John Travolta's gooned-out character, Vincent, takes Mia Wallace (Uma Thurman), the wife of his gangster boss Marcellus Wallace out to dinner at the behest of Marcellus, Vincent begins to sense a flirtatious vibe from her that definitely spells trouble. As in, the last guy who deigned to give Mrs. Wallace a foot massage was thrown out a window. However, Vincent, who now considers himself stuck between a rock and a hard place (it wouldn't be prudent to turn Mrs. Wallace down and hurt her feelings either) has no idea what he's really in for; while Vincent's in the bathroom, Mrs. Wallace discovers his ultra-pure heroin stash in his jacket pocket and inhales a line. Vincent returns from the bathroom to find Mrs. Wallace unconscious and fading fast, which prompts a call to his dealer from the phone in his car.

Now this scene has everything that makes for heart-palpitating (no pun intended) excitement – high stakes (Mrs. Wallace's potential death) and higher stakes (Vincent's assured death, should Wallace's wife expire while on his clock), which sets the scene beautifully as Vincent arrives at the home of his dealer (played by Eric Stoltz) at three o' clock in the morning, desperate for a shot of adrenaline that will jumpstart Mrs. Wallace's heart and bring her back – literally – from the dead. But what makes the scene especially memorable (in a film chock full of memorable scenes, no less) is the simultaneous combination of humor and horror that Tarantino is able to infuse into the moment. Both the dealer and Vincent are concerned primarily with saving their own skins, and we find ourselves truly empathizing for their plight, despite their irrefutable status as the kinds of lowlifes you would avoid like the plague if you were ever to encounter them in real life. And yet amidst all their fumbling desperation – their arguments about the consequences of Mrs. Wallace's death, their inability to figure out how to handle the shot of adrenaline correctly – lies genuine concern for the welfare of the girl who is lying on death's door right in front of them.

When they are successful in administering the shot, there is a kind of heroism – albeit mitigated somewhat – that is redemptive, which again addresses the theme of the film. *Pulp Fiction* is, for all its well-deserved kudos for unique visual style and intricate, fractured narrative structure, a simple tale about the redemption of hoodlums. Vincent (and to a lesser degree, his dealer) is redeemed by his actions which, although he doesn't realize it until later, if ever, wind up getting him out of the sticky situation in which he had found himself. However temporary his redemption is (he ends up shot dead on a toilet seat), it is nonetheless sufficient to give him a moment of pause in a life that has known little other than knee-jerk survival tactics.

3. *Jacob's Ladder* – Angels and Demons: Jacob, the character played by Tim Robbins in the 1990 film *Jacob's Ladder*, returns from Vietnam only to find that strange things are afoot. Haunted by his memories of the war (as well as of the death of one of his sons, played by a young Macaulay Culkin, prior to the war), and separated from his wife, he has tried to begin life anew as a mild-mannered postal employee. However he soon finds himself tortured by continuous visions of diabolical, hellish creatures. To make matters worse, the men he had been fighting with in Vietnam (whom we saw exhibiting bizarre behavior in the film's first scene) are also beginning to experience strange hallucinations.

The film ultimately builds to a twist ending that, while not entirely logical, drives home a spiritually powerful message about life and death. En route, we are treated to a scene between Jacob and his good-hearted chiropractor, played by Danny Aiello, who tells Jacob something he'd read about angels and devils. "When you're dying," Aiello says, "all the unresolved business of your life comes out. And if you're fighting it, if you're still unresolved about it, these visions appear as demons. But if you've made your peace, you look closer and realize that the demons are really angels."

As Jacob draws closer and closer to the moment of truth that ends the movie, he realizes that the demonic visions that have plagued him are, in fact, the unresolved issues pertaining to not only the death of his son but of his own impending death as well. Jacob learns to let go, and as he walks toward the light at the top of a flight of stairs, his hand in that of his dead son's, we realize that what we have been watching all along is a meditation on life and death and the stage in between – and that Danny Aiello's character has provided us with the film's bittersweet but uplifting theme.

4. *Almost Famous* – Lester Bangs Explains It All: In Cameron Crowe's semi-autobiographical film "Almost Famous," a fourteen year-old boy named William Miller (played by Patrick Fugit) in the mid-1970s gets the opportunity to go on the road with a rising rock band called Stillwater (reputedly a cross between the Allman Brothers Band and Led Zeppelin, both of whom Crowe covered). During the course of his journey, William enjoys all the standard perks associated with coming of age – he falls in love with a beautiful groupie played by Kate Hudson, in her breakout role – as well as some of the downsides associated with growing up; the band he has so faithfully covered winds up betraying William to the magazine that has hired him, thus killing the story. It is in this final blow that the movie's theme – that rock and roll, in the truest sense, died in the 1970's when it became corporate big money – plays out.

The theme, like all good themes, is stated in the film's first act; in this case, by the character of famed rock critic and commentator Lester Bangs (played by Philip Seymour Hoffman). William is walking by a radio station one day when he sees Bangs chatting up a deejay about rock poseurs versus true rock gods. William then asks Bangs for advice during a walk the two take together, at which point Bangs tells William never to get too close to the subjects you're covering. More importantly, he waxes nostalgic about the good old days of rock and roll without sounding like a washed-up cliché, then expounds on what has killed the music business – namely the bands' compliance with the corporate mentality (symbolized by the labels and, later in the movie, the big bucks manager that comes to woo Stillwater away from their longtime – and small-time – manager).

The evocation of time and place and how it pertains to theme is beautifully alluded to in this scene, but because the film is truly about the dangers of blind compliance – the bands with the labels, William with the bands, William with his overprotective mother – Bangs is giving William advice that is not only thematic, but will also be of service to him long after this magical time has come and gone. Crowe's deft handling of the material speaks volumes about his considerable abilities as a true craftsman; a lesser writer might have used Bangs' acerbic voice to deliver a one-note rant that simply encompassed the issues pertaining to the film's portrayal of a time and place that was slipping away. Instead there is a gentleness in Bangs's message that in no way mitigates or does a disservice to the writings and philosophy of the real-life Lester Bangs. Crowe sees the big picture and understands the complex shadings of the universe of which he writes; as a result, he delivers a scene that is about much more than it purportedly seems.

5. *Training Day* – Ever Had Your Shit Pushed In?: The Antoine Fuqua-directed, David Ayer-scripted 2001 film "Training Day" is a masterfully-written drama that delves deep within the ambivalence felt by police as far as what lines they will and will not cross. In the course of one day, Officer Jake Hoyt (played by Ethan Hawke) is pushed to the limits of his ethical and physical endurance by Alonzo (played by Denzel Washington, who received his second Academy Award for the role), the superior for whom he (initially) wishes to work. Following a scene in which Alonzo, Hoyt, and a group of other officers break into the home of Alonzo's onetime mentor Roger (played by Scott Glenn, to whom we'd been introduced earlier in the film) simply to rob him of some "dirty" money, Hoyt questions what it is precisely he has signed up for.

Alonzo delivers a speech about the shifting of the moral line, how he too started off like Hoyt, but that these are the necessary steps cops like him take in the course of self-preservation. Hoyt listens, but it's clear that Alonzo realizes that his protege isn't really hearing what's been said. So Alonzo takes Hoyt over to a gang house, under the auspices of dropping a few things off. Alonzo disappears into the bathroom, at which point Hoyt is cajoled by three Latino gangbangers to join them in a game of cards.

It is in this scene that Ayer proves himself to be a master of dialogue, character, and situation. From the moment we meet the three gangsters, we get a sense for their differences; the leader is named Smiley and never smiles, another bobs up and down, hopped-up on the prospect of violence and, most likely, a whole host of illicit pharmaceuticals, while still another smiles continuously but has the unyielding hint of just-around-the-corner malevolence dancing around the corners of his eyes.

The scene starts out innocently enough; Hoyt stands by the door, waiting for Alonzo, but is informed by Smiley that Alonzo is "taking a shit" and will be awhile. Hoyt then sits down and is dealt a hand. The gangster with the darting eyes asks him – with a smile, natch – how long he's been a pig. Hoyt, unfazed, retorts that he's been a pig for a few months, then takes some cards. Hoyt's hand turns out to be the winning one (although the hopped-up gangbanger mistakenly believes that his two pair is the winning hand). Though the threat of malice hovers through the scene, somehow the gangbangers come off just jovial enough to lower Hoyt's defenses; the gangster who'd asked Hoyt how long he'd been a pig asks to see Hoyt's gun. When Hoyt blanches, he tells Hoyt that it's okay – just take out the bullets. Hoyt does and slides the piece over to him. We are then told the reason why Alonzo needed the money – that he'd killed a Russian gangster in Las Vegas the weekend prior and that the Russian mob told Alonzo that he owed them a million dollars before midnight of the present day.

The gangsters frame this information in an admiring sense; Alonzo might be ruthless, but they respect that. But without the audience realizing it, they have also yielded a key piece of information that motivates Alonzo's actions so that they appear, if not justified, at least understandable. The gangsters then ask Hoyt if he's ever had his shit pushed in – presumably a reference to prison-and assure him that they've all had their shit pushed in. Smiley, who has been silent for most of the scene (but is assuredly, without uttering a word, the most seasoned sociopath of the three), eyes Hoyt.

The malice in the air now grows, as Smiley tsk-tsks and tells Hoyt that it looks as though Alonzo took off. Hoyt looks out the window; sure enough, Alonzo's car is gone. The color now drains from Hoyt's face as he realizes that this entire scene has been a set-up – payback for not having gone along with Alonzo's scheme to rip off Roger and split the booty. Hoyt, now left without a gun, upends the table and tries to fight his way out, but he's overcome by the gangsters, who drag him down the hall and dump him in the bathtub. Hoyt is about to be shot, when Smiley spots a girl's wallet (earlier, Hoyt had saved a young girl from being raped by crackheads in an alley). Hoyt, staring down the barrel of a shotgun, tells Smiley how he came to possess the wallet, and Smiley calls the girl, who happens to be his cousin. She confirms Hoyt's story, and Smiley hangs up. Then he pulls Hoyt up from the bathtub and gives him a reprieve, thanking him for saving his cousin.

As Hoyt prepares to leave, Smiley makes a point of telling him that the fact that they were about to kill him had nothing to do with anything personal; it was just business. And it is this coda – or button – to an emotionally exhausting (and almost 10-minute-long) sequence that gives it one final beat of punctuation; Smiley and his group may be killers and criminals, but they follow a code of loyalty and, above all else, don't regard what they do as particularly cruel. It's just "business," which in the course of this extremely well-written scene somehow makes sense.

With this script, Ayer provides the fledgling screenwriter with an excellent example of how to build a scene to a climax without downplaying its underlying tension; how to quickly establish three memorable characters whom we will never see again in the film; and how to weave in some crucial information without loading the scene down with expositional bloat.

GETTING HIRED

Film Schools/Formal Screenwriting Programs

CHAPTER 6

The Film School Model

In the late 1960s and early 1970s, film school enjoyed a renaissance. With the new aesthetic in Hollywood (a period, described in Peter Biskind's excellent book – and documentary – *Easy Riders and Raging Bulls*, 2nd commonly referred to as Hollywood's second "Golden Era") pushing the increasingly accepted notion that film could be art, film school – once considered a bohemian curiosity – became a legitimate form of scholarly pursuit virtually overnight. High-profile film school graduates such as Martin Scorsese and Francis Ford Coppola, who studiously emulated European filmmakers like Jean-Luc Godard and Eric Rohmer (as well as stalwarts like Bergman and Fellini) began turning out films like *The Godfather* and *Taxi Driver*. Although this had probably more to do with an increased permissiveness on the part of the studios, whose creaky, old-fashioned style of filmmaking had practically bankrupted them in the wake of society's progressive aesthetic demands, film schools – which were ultimately divided into two programs, film production (directors) and film writing (screenwriters) – were nonetheless seen as a fertile breeding ground for cutting-edge talent.

But how relevant is the film school model today, given the current studio mandate that recruits much of its talent from the training grounds of commercials and music videos (and, on the writing end, from the worlds of fiction and playwriting)? And being accepted to one of the better programs in the first place is hardly a lock, given that the competition to get in is on a par with some of the nation's finest law and medical schools. So what other forms of professional training can you look into that might provide you not only with some valuable writing experience, but also those necessary contacts that will help you get your foot in the door once it comes time to send your material around? And are there any other ways to get yourself noticed – contests, fellowships and the like – where the panelists are respected members of the industry who might take note of an especially talented writer and help promote her cause?

The answer to all of these questions, fortunately, is yes: there are methodical ways of going about building a career. It isn't all talent or all luck, but if you use the guidance in the chapters that follow, you will greatly increase your chances of getting read and ultimately finding some measure of success in this business.

The Film School Decision

One of the side effects of the increased demand for a film school education has been an increase in the number of film schools offering what they claim is a professional-quality level of education. While some programs are indeed respectable enough, it is important to remember that the best film school programs will employ active (or at least recently active) members of the entertainment community. Since those members almost always live in Los Angeles or New York – primarily Los Angeles, which remains the capital of the entertainment industry – most reputable programs will be located in striking distance of these two cities. In this regard, screenwriting is unlike fiction writing; Iowa and Stanford garnered glowing reviews for their masters' programs in fiction writing due largely in part to the novelist's proclivity to live in less urban surroundings, but with few exceptions this is simply not the case in the world of screenwriters, most of whom live in or around L.A. Even writers whose careers have tailed off a bit tend to stick nearby with the hopes of a – not entirely unlikely, given the natural ebbs and flows one tends to find in most screenwriting careers – comeback, a disproving thumb-of-the-nose to Fitzgerald's once-widely-accepted notion that "there are no second acts in American life."

So where can, or should, you go to film school? Well, before you take that step, ask yourself this: are you ready to drop everything and treat this career change with the same discipline and determination you would a new career in law or medicine? Because if you are not, then you truly have no business attending film school. Which is not to say that there isn't a writing program in which you could enroll (more on that later), but film school itself is a serious commitment; even if you are attending with the express purpose of becoming a professional screenwriter, you will be expected to take classes in all film-related subjects (production, critical analysis, television and video, etc.) in pursuit of earning your MFA – Master of Fine Arts – degree.

Yes, there are tremendous rewards to attending film school; not only will you invariably find the education fascinating, you will also come into contact with some of the best and brightest film minds in the country, all of whom have been subjected to the same rigorous admission requirements that you faced on your way in. Forging a successful film partnership with a simpatico soul is not only a realistic goal, it should be one of your primary objectives; one need look no further than the example set forth by Alexander Payne and Jim Taylor, who shared the Academy Award for Best Adapted Screenplay for their work on the film *Sideways* several years and successful collaborations after both were MFA students at UCLA.

The "Big Five" Film Schools

Which brings us back to our initial question: provided you meet all the pertinent lifestyle criteria and have a competitive writing sample (ideally a play or screenplay, but admissions committees have been known to evaluate fiction or non-fiction samples as well), where should you apply? Just as the Ivy League has its "Big Three," the world of film schools has its "Big Five," which are listed below, in alphabetical order.

1. **American Film Institute (AFI):** AFI did not used to be a conventionally-structured Master of Fine Arts Program, but in recent years this has changed; graduates have the option of applying for a degree or of pursuing a certificate of completion option. AFI's program, located at the American Film Institute, whose campus is at the edge of the Hollywood Hills-adjacent neighborhood of Los Feliz, is one the entertainment industry's most prized institutions (the AFI list of the top 100 films of all time is considered one of the industry's gold standards, and their lifetime achievement award dinners attract a luminous, A-List set of attendees). AFI's faculty includes such industry luminaries as Frank Pierson, who in addition to having written the Sidney Lumet-directed classic *Dog Day Afternoon*, is the current president of the Academy of Motion Picture Arts and Sciences (whose members determine the Academy Awards). To read more about AFI, log onto their website at www.afi.com.

2. **Columbia University:** Past film school deans have included such industry titans as Milos Forman, and the combination of a prime New York location and Ivy League pedigree has continuously allowed Columbia to attract some of the most prestigious names in the film industry, such as James Schamus, who runs Focus Features (Universal's specialty, or small-film arm) in addition to writing films like *The Ice Storm*, *Crouching Tiger, Hidden Dragon*, and *The Hulk*, to name a few. Columbia boasts seven of the last eight student academy award film recipients and has garnered a well-deserved reputation for integrating storytelling into the visual medium of film. Columbia's film school does not require prospective students to take the GRE exam. To learn more about Columbia's film school, go to their website at www.arts.columbia.edu/film/.

3. **New York University:** NYU's Tisch School of the Arts was founded in 1965 and includes such alumni as Jim Jarmusch, Spike Lee, and M. Night Shyamalan. NYU embraces its "downtown" reputation and embraces avant- garde filmmakers and writers but, as evidenced by its eclectic faculty, list of alumni, and long list of produced film and television credits, it hardly eschews the mainstream. NYU does not require prospective students to take the GRE exam. To learn more about NYU's Tisch School of the Arts, visit their website at: www.tisch.nyu.edu.

4. **University of California at Los Angeles (UCLA):** UCLA's film school benefits from its proximity to the entertainment industry, and its first-rate screenwriting program has turned out such names as Neal Jiminez (*The River's Edge*, *The Waterdance*) and Scott Rosenberg (*Beautiful Girls*, *Con Air*) among others. Due to UCLA's reputation as one of the premier institutions in which to learn how to write mainstream films, agents and other industry representatives always seem to be accessible; what's more, the fluid interaction the school encourages between student filmmakers and student writers enables plenty of relationship-building within the school's walls. UCLA does, however, require all prospective students to take the GRE exam. For more information about UCLA, their website is: www.tft.ucla.edu.

5. **University of Southern California (USC):** USC boasts perhaps the most famous film school in the country, and with alumni and benefactors such as Steven Spielberg, George Lucas, and Robert Zemeckis, it is no mystery as to why. If USC has one drawback, it is that for all the acclaim its directors' program has enjoyed, there has been little mention made of its screenwriting department. This is unjustified: USC's screenwriting department benefits from the same proximity to the industry as UCLA (although its decidedly less-than-tony neighborhood is a far cry from UCLA's prime Westwood setting), and its faculty is every bit as distinguished as UCLA's. For more information about USC's film school, their website is www.cntv.usc.edu.

Screenwriting Extension Programs

If you aren't able to make a full-time commitment to film school – and most people don't have that luxury – the good news is that between local night school and the internet, there will almost assuredly be a writing program in which you can take part. The downside to most local night schools is that, just like with many film programs, if they are not located within striking range of Los Angeles or New York they simply don't have access to quality professional screenwriters. You should always look up any prospective teacher on an internet search engine and see if they have any credits; websites like IMDB (the Internet Movie Database, a comprehensive film website) won't be as helpful in this department; they tend to list only produced credits, and there are numerous talented writers who, as a result of the vicissitudes of the movie business, have sold several projects without having had anything produced. But Google will list any mention of that writer's sales if they were ever published, which most of them are in some way, and will probably have some other links for you to follow in order to complete your research.

The programs listed above, with the exception of AFI, all have extension programs that are the equivalent of continuing education whose writing departments are manned by writers of some repute (UCLA's is especially strong). What these extension programs offer that film schools don't is online courses, complete with virtual chat rooms and professors' virtual office hours, which permit you to treat your education in the same way you would a correspondence course. You might weigh these facts prior to enrolling in a local, or lesser film school (which is never cheap, mind you) whose faculty and resources will inevitably be inferior to those offered by the extension programs of the big five.

Screenwriting Fellowships, Contests and Pitch Festivals

Screenwriting fellowships

Let's say that film school isn't an option for you, and that maybe you took a class or two online but that too didn't yield any industry avenue openings. If you are convinced that your lack of recognition is truly unwarranted, there are fellowship programs that range from little more than contests to actual in-house "gigs" that, should you be fortunate enough to receive one, will guarantee you a great deal of immediate industry recognition.

1. **The Chesterfield Writer's Film Project:** Based out of Paramount Pictures with help from Steven Spielberg's Amblin Pictures, the Chesterfield Fellowship awards five winners a stipend of $20,000 and pairs them up with a screenwriting mentor. The program's mentors are some of the industry's best-known and well-respected writers and have included such names as Steven Zaillian (*Schindler's List*) and David Koepp (*Spider*

Man, The War Of The Worlds). Past Chesterfield recipients have sold projects to practically every studio, network, and cable station in the industry. To apply, log onto their website at: www.chesterfield-co.com.

2. **The Nicholl Fellowship:** Presented by the Academy of Motion Picture Arts and Sciences, the Don and Gee Nicholl Fellowship Award is awarded to five winners per year and entails a $30,000 dollar stipend. While Nicholl fellows do not participate in any one-on-one mentorship program, the award itself serves as sufficient validation that they are ready to start their careers, and the vast majority of producers and agents in town will happily return a phone call from a Nicholl's fellowship awardee. To find out more about the Nicholl's fellowship, log on to their website at: www.oscars.org/nicholl//

3. **The IFP MSP McKnight Artist Fellowship for Screenwriters:** These awards are given out by the McKnight foundation and are located in Minneapolis, and acknowledge "Minnesota artists for accomplishments in writing for the screen as demonstrated by one completed feature screenplay." McKnight fellows are compensated with a $25,000 stipend (up from the former amount of $10,000) and are given professional encouragement and recognition from the McKnight foundation. For eligibility and details, log on to their website at: www.mcknight.org/arts/fellowships.aspx.

4. **The Writer's Arc:** A new, not-for-profit program founded by a former studio executive and a producer (and sponsored by numerous industry heavyweights), The Writer's Arc pays its recipients $10,000 to come to L.A. to write, network, and learn. The Writer's Arc accepts five fellows bi-yearly and engages them for twenty-week sessions. For more information, log on to their website at www.writersarc.org.

Screenwriting contests

Screenwriting contests are a bit different from screenwriting fellowships in that they award a one-time cash prize instead of a combination of stipend and mentorship support. Still, many of these contests are quite prestigious (not to mention financially lucrative) and can yield the kind of exposure you'll need to get your career on track. One such possibility is the UCLA Extension Screenplay Competition, an opportunity for three outstanding Writers' Program students to gain industry exposure, individual mentoring and training, and cash prizes. Winners receive $1,000 (1st place), $500 (2nd place) and $250 (3rd place); a guaranteed read by an agent, producer, and/or creative executive; a one-on-one script consultation ($700 value) with a professional screenwriter prior to the final judging; and a logline listing on Baseline Spec Market. You can download a submission packet at their website (www.uclaextension.edu/writers), or call the UCLA Extension Writer's Program directly at (310) 825-9415. For a comprehensive list of screenwriting contests and the kinds of awards they offer, log on to: www.filmmakers.com/contests/directory.htm.

Pitch festivals

You've submitted your script to all the fellowships and contests around, but you've still gotten nowhere. If only someone could hear your idea and get a sense of your passion for your project, you're convinced that you'd get a leg-up over the competition. If this sounds like what's going on with you, chances are you'd benefit from one of the pitch festivals that are held from time to time in Los Angeles. A pitch festival is essentially an open audition, where writers wait in line to pitch their ideas to agents, managers, and production companies. The lines can be endless, but at least you'll get heard. New pitch festivals pop up from time to time, but the stalwarts of the group are:

- **The Fade In PowerPitch Fest:** Held at a hotel in Hollywood and generally considered to be the most well-organized and best-attended of all the pitchfests. For registration information, look them up on their website at: www.fadeinonline.com/Contests/EventChoose.html
- **The ShowBiz Data Worldwide Pitch Festival:** This one differs from the others in that you are required to submit a two-to-five minute video of your pitch. For submission information, look them up at www.showbizdata.com.
- **The Hollywood Film Festival's "Sell Your Story to Hollywood Buyers" Conference:** An extensive weekend that would benefit anyone with the money and resources to attend. For information, log on to their website at: www.hollywoodfestival.com/sell_your_story.html

Although these festivals are sometimes referred to (not entirely unfairly) as *The Gong Show*, they have also yielded stories of successful sales and networking opportunities that have kept them in business for a long time. A word to the wise: most of the "executives" you'll be meeting will be fairly low-level, and some will actually be assistants. However, the lower-end people in the business are often the hungriest, and what they may lack in title they'll more than make up for in hustle and contact information.

Alternate Strategies for Getting In

CHAPTER 7

Hiring Script Consultants

Let's say you've applied to film school and were rejected not only at every turn, but also from every contest and fellowship to which you applied as well. Despite this strong vote of non-confidence, you firmly believe that your script deserves professional consideration. Maybe all it needs is an objective, seasoned set of eyes that will hone in on whatever is still missing and help you fix it. But what can you do if don't know anyone personally who fits this description?

The good news is that you can hire the services of a freelance script consultant to evaluate your script for a fee – usually between $500 and $1,000, depending on the scope of services you request. Because the evaluation of the creative arts is such a subjective area – and because of the degree of closeness you can feel for your material – you have to make sure that you're hiring these people for the express purpose of helping you get your script closer to submission quality. Which is why the first thing you should ask a prospective script consultant (and you are well within your rights to conduct at least a mini-interview; keep in mind that most of these people, the quality ones anyway, welcome the money and will be more than happy to prove their worthiness) is "will you tell me if I'm not really in the ballpark?" Because chances are that the first few times you attempt to write a script, you might be so far off the mark that the most ethical thing a professional writer can do for you at this stage is offer some nurturing – but very broad – tips for a minimal amount of money.

Provided you wish to proceed and that both parties feel the script is worthy of a more in-depth critical analysis, you would be well-advised to run your most comprehensive personality and compatibility test on the prospective script consultant – the same type of test or drill you would use when hiring a tutor or anyone else who makes money off an intellectual craft. For example, does the consultant inspire you and help you see the big picture, or do you feel confused and more than a bit intimidated? Try to get a feeling for how his sensibilities will mesh with yours; you are, after all, bringing this person into something far more intimate than a mortgage. And make sure that the consultant in question has at least a few credits – accepting that most will be fairly dated, but understanding that any screenwriter who has a decent grasp of craft and has provided this kind of service for others will be immensely helpful to you in your goal of becoming a professional screenwriter.

If you're not the kind of person who has the time or the patience for a comprehensive search, several of the extension programs listed above offer a one-on-one script doctor option (UCLA's resources in this department are especially good; contact the Writer's Extension office at 31-206-2612). As you would with anyone else, however, it's never a bad idea to run the prospective name through a search engine. Also, keep in mind that in the vast majority of cases a script consultant will not be a direct conduit into the business, and unless you find yourselves striking up a professional relationship (rare, but not unheard of) you would be crossing a line to ask them for their contacts.

Q&A: Matt Roshkow, Script Consultant

Matt Roshkow, a screenwriter with several produced credits to his name, had the following advice to give to fledgling writers:

What's the difference between you and a script doctor?

A script doctor is a highly-paid screenwriter who is employed by studios to rewrite scripts that are in trouble. They differ from the average rewrite assignee in that a script doctor usually isn't called in until a movie is weeks (or sometimes days) away from going into production and the script still has significant problems. An independent script consultant is someone who provides services to up-and-coming (and in some cases, professional) writers, similar to the way editors-for-hire provide their services in the publishing world. Some script consultants refer to themselves as script doctors, but the semantics aren't really important (although, as a writer myself, I probably shouldn't admit that!)

What are those services, exactly?

Depends. Sometimes it can be as simple as evaluating an outline and giving the writer tips on how to make their story work better. Mostly, however, I read finished scripts and help make them better.

What does a script consultant typically charge?

Usually between $500 and $1,000, depending on the scope of services and the consultant's experience and track record. Some consultants charge top dollar for just a read and a page or two of notes, but they've usually got a list of success stories a mile long on their webpage.

Who would benefit the most from a script consultant?

A writer who has written a few scripts and is starting to get a grasp on the basic tenets of the craft. Even though your instincts will tell you to rush out there with the first thing you've ever written, you'd probably be wasting your money if you brought that one to a consultant. Because in the vast majority of cases, it'll be a mess. Where people like me can really make a difference is if your script is in the ballpark, professionally speaking, and what it needs is some focus and streamlining.

How important should a consultant's credits be to your decision whether or not to choose him or her?

Very... and not at all. Obviously, you shouldn't go with someone whose bluster hides the fact that he or she has never really worked as a screenwriter; it's like those *How To Sell Your Spec Script For A Million Dollars* books written by writers who've never sold one. And yet some writers with fewer credits are far better communicators than other writers with several. The key is to do some research and find a consultant who you feel will be able to help make your script better.

Any other advice you have for beginning writers?

Yes. Don't let your ego stand in the way. Try to divorce yourself emotionally as much as possible from the fact that a complete stranger is essentially telling you that your baby has warts. Because it does, no matter how many of them you've created or how beautiful you think they are. Every script could use some advice on how to improve it, and the more open-minded you are to hearing it, the better the end result will be.

Script Reading and Other Industry Jobs

Probably the best way in which you can help your professional cause – particularly if you are a recent college graduate and have some way to make the financial side of an unpaid internship work – is to accept a low-level job in the entertainment industry. Hollywood lore is replete with stories of famous careers started in agency mailrooms, although most of these people wound up on the business end of the business. For an aspiring writer, there is no better place to begin a career than as a script reader for a studio or production company.

A script reader's duties entail reading scripts that have been submitted to the studio or production company and writing coverage, which is a specialized industry template that includes a summary of the film's plot, an evaluation that describes why you did or didn't like it, and a breakdown of ratings – poor, fair, good, excellent – of such script components as character, dialogue, and story. The reader then decides whether or not to recommend the script and/or the writer; often a reader will recommend the script for purchase for commercial reasons, but will not recommend the writer; similarly, there are times when a reader will pass on a writer's script for commercial reasons, but will recommend the writer for consideration for future assignments. Finally the reader passes the scripts that fall into the recommend pile along to the next rung up the ladder. Although these jobs are hard to get (and don't pay terribly well to boot), there is no doubt that you will learn volumes about the industry's tastes and simultaneously receive an irreplaceable education in the craft of screenwriting by getting a chance to do nothing but read and analyze scripts for the better part of your working day… and night, as is often the case.

If you can't get a job as a script reader, you should try to get a job doing anything industry-related. Log on to everything from studio websites (run a Google search under their names, i.e., Universal Studios, Paramount Studios, etc.) to Craig's List (www.craigslist.org), the latter of which also features actual writing jobs that, depending on the samples and experience required, you might actually qualify for. Do whatever you can to get your foot in the door all while continuing to develop your craft as a writer; just remember that if you have the requisite talent and drive, the rest will follow.

Confessions of an Industry Reader

- If you have any irrational worries that I'll steal your idea, fear not. If I steal your idea, your agent (to ensure quality control and due to legal stipulations, production entities accept only agent-represented submissions) will make sure that information makes the rounds; given how small a town this really is, it'll spell curtains for my career.
- If you have any irrational worries that I won't pass your script along out of jealousy, again fear not. In the event that your script becomes

the hottest read in the business, I'll get handed my walking paper before I've had time to even rescue it from the discard pile.

- I love movies; always have. Make me remember why with every page you write.
- I got my first script reading job through Craig's List; from there I kept my eyes open and my ears to the ground when it came to better opportunities, which finally landed me in this position.
- I read about 10 to 15 scripts per weekend, and more during the week. Don't adorn your script with any cute props, but make sure you've got my attention pretty early on. I've tossed scripts into the "reject" pile by page three, so make sure your page one grab, page ten grab (a "grab" is a moment that lets the reader know that the script has something going for it and ensures that the reader will continue to read on), and first act break are memorable.
- Make sure you CAPITALIZE any important actions or visuals whenever you're writing action or narrative. And try not to break up action and narrative into two-to-three line blocks; if you're curious why, try reading your own action at eleven at night after a 14-hour day reading other material.
- If you want to get a job doing what I'm doing, re-read the third point I made – the one about loving movies – and make sure that you agree with it one hundred and twenty five percent.

Networking and Schmoozing

Even though the adage, "it's all about who you know" (and what they're willing to do for you) is an overly simplistic assessment of the entertainment industry, there is no doubt that having good professional relationships can only help when it comes time to send your material around. But how can you go about making those all-important contacts? If you live in Los Angeles or New York (but primarily if you live in Los Angeles), chances are you will have some decent opportunities to rub shoulders with people who can ultimately be of assistance to you; avoid "hot" industry hangouts and clubs and instead focus on more intimate gatherings, such as the functions sponsored by the Writer's Guild (you don't necessarily have to be a member to attend) or college alumni industry-related events (virtually every Ivy

League school has an alumni organization in this area, as do schools heavy in the communications fields like Northwestern, Syracuse, and Emerson).

If you can't join these organizations yourself for whatever reason, try to hook up with friends and acquaintances who can, and then go with them. Keep your ear to the ground about industry-related parties and do whatever you can to wrangle an invite to the multitude of these affairs that are thrown by entertainment assistants; remember, within the next few years many of these people will be executives who can be of great assistance to your writing career.

Keep in mind, however, that your agenda should never be connection first, personality second; if you don't naturally jibe with someone, it will be every bit as obvious to them as it is to you. Try to remember that this is, when all is said and done, show business, replete with a multitude of engaging and animated personalities who fled more stable careers. Which means that it shouldn't be too much of an effort to make friends, and that you should generally be compatible with the people with whom you wish to establish relationships; it will give them greater incentive to help you out in the future if they genuinely like you. Find common interests – sports, for example. You'd be surprised at the number of writers who got critical meetings off of informal games of softball, basketball, beach volleyball, or hockey. Join a rotisserie league. Play poker – a current rage in Hollywood – with whomever you can, knowing that one game can lead to another, and before you know it you could be sitting at a table next to Ben Affleck (who probably won't be of much assistance to you, but at least you'll get to tell everyone back home).

If you do not live in Los Angeles or New York and haven't found your online classes to be a bonanza of contacts, try to enter as many of the aforementioned competitions as you can, especially the pitch festivals (even if it requires saving money that would be wiser spent on groceries or rent). Employ every trick in the book you can think of to get people on the phone. Remember that at the end of the day, if your work is undeniably good, someone will eventually take notice as they did for Ehren Kruger, a guy with no connections or "ins" to start but who found himself perched at the top of the A-list of screenwriters in a relatively short time.

Ehren Kruger's Journey from Unknown to A-List Screenwriter

Ehren Kruger, who is perhaps best known for adapting the Japanese horror film *Ringu* into the American smash hit *The Ring*, first came on Hollywood's radar with the release of the 1999 film *Arlington Road*, which was based on a spec script he'd written. Kruger had entered *Arlington Road* in the prestigious Nicholl Fellowship contest (see Chapter 5) and won, which sparked a flurry of interest from studios and producers. Despite the heat, however, nobody bought the script until an independent producer took it around town and matched it up with a director, Mark Pellington, with whom buyers wanted to be in business. Soon Tim Robbins and Jeff Bridges came on board and the film was financed and released.

Kruger notes that *Arlington Road* was hardly the first script he'd ever written. "I started trying to write screenplays when I was in high school," he notes. "Emphasis on trying." Kruger, who then went on to attend NYU as an undergraduate, estimates that he wrote about ten scripts before attempting to get an agent with one, adding that he read as many professional-caliber scripts as he could get his hands on and waited until his own work was at that level. "Had I tried to get my career going based upon the earliest scripts I wrote, (industry) doors would have closed in my face real quick."

Once *Arlington Road* was set up, Kruger next sold his script *Reindeer Games* to Miramax's Dimension Films division. Although the ensuing film, which struck many as an unwieldy blend of *Reservoir Dogs* and *It's A Wonderful Life*, didn't set the box office on fire, Kruger was awarded a multi-picture deal with Dimension. As part of that deal, Kruger was asked to write the third installment in the *Scream* series. The success of that movie led to several other writing assignments, including *The Ring*, which grossed about a quarter of a billion dollars worldwide. His current slate includes the sequel to *The Ring*, (which, Kruger notes, is far different from the sequel to *Ringu II*), a Southern Gothic spookfest called *The Skeleton Key*, and a retelling of the lives of the most famous fairy-tale concocters of all time called *The Brothers Grimm*, which is being directed by Terry Gilliam of *12 Monkeys* fame.

Kruger's success serves as a mild rebuke to the notion that who you rub shoulders with is a critical determinant of ultimate success (Kruger lives in San Francisco and only ventures down to Hollywood for meetings, but has been known to fly to the set of his movies for additional script work). His success is proof that at the end of the day a screenwriter can succeed on the basis of talent, good judgment, and sound commercial instincts.

ON THE JOB

Agents for Screenwriters

CHAPTER 8

Budd Schulberg's 1941 satirical Hollywood novel *What Makes Sammy Run?* first introduced the world to Sammy Glick, an agent with a spectacular skill for self-advancement that often came at the expense of those around him. The soulless, shameless huckster became a symbol for a segment of the industry that has, more often than not, been maligned by everyone familiar with their tactics. And yet even though the stereotypical agent can be seamlessly inserted into the punchline of virtually any lawyer joke ("Why don't sharks eat agents? Professional courtesy"), the truth is that creative types like writers need agents. Which is not to say that the alliance between the two parties is blissful – indeed, to hear each side air its laundry list of complaints about the other is to truly understand the definition of the phrase "dysfunctional relationship." But even the greenest writer is well aware that he who represents himself represents a fool. Therefore, if you are ever going to succeed as a writer, you will have to have an agent.

But what type of agent will be right for you, and what kind of agency will he be a part of? For although the image of Sammy Glick may still be alive and well, the business of agenting has changed quite a bit. It is extremely difficult to interest an agent in your work, and yet even if you're lucky enough for this to be the case, the agent in question may not ultimately be the best person to represent you.

What is An Agent?

An agent is basically a headhunter for an artist – in this case you, the writer. Their job is to either sell the original spec scripts you write or to get you work at the studios based on your scripts, which they are constantly circulating around town in order to win you fans among the executives and producers in charge of hiring writers for writing assignments. Agents work entirely on commission, taking ten percent of whatever fee they can negotiate for your work, thus the origin of the term "tenpercenteries," used in *Variety* and *The Hollywood Reporter* to describe the boutiques and major agencies for whom they work. Keep in mind that it is unheard of for an agent to charge more than ten percent of your earnings; similarly, it is out of the question for an agent to demand an upfront fee. If these are the terms being presented by someone claiming to be an agent, you should avoid them at all costs.

Because agents initially work for free, it is imperative that they feel passionately about the work they represent. Some agents make lofty assurances about their choosiness when signing clients, but have developed a reputation in the business for doing the "spaghetti thing" (ie: throwing as much up against the wall to see what will stick).

While the numbers game might be fine for anything that boils down to mere statistics, it does not benefit any writer, whose work is often likened to "their baby," to be treated like a number on a roulette table. For agents' reputations throughout the industry are forged not only on the way in which they do business, but on their word and their taste in talent as well. If an agent calls an executive to rave about a new writer, chances are the executive will think back to the last recommended writers proffered forth by the agent. And if most of those recommendations were a waste of the executive's time, you can bet that the writer being pitched will not get read anytime soon.

How Do You Get An Agent?

Because agents are viewed as the gateway to the big brass ring (and for good reason), they tend to be besieged by phone calls and queries from people with designs on making it in the film business. Given the sheer volume – not to mention questionable, at times, sanity – of this segment of the population, it is small wonder that agents sequester themselves behind their assistants. And given their very real time constraints, there are only so many calls and e-mails to which they can respond-the odds are that when an agent scans his or her call log, they simply delete any unfamiliar names. Sending them your script unsolicited is a waste of time, even if you attach a bouquet of flowers, a box of chocolate, or front row tickets for that agent's favorite basketball team (all of which aspiring writers have done) for the simple reason that agencies have been sued far too many times by unrepresented writers who claim their script was stolen. The way the agencies see it, the risk that they may be discarding the next *Chinatown* is far outweighed by some very real liability concerns.

So how do you get an agent? Below are a few tips that, while certainly no guarantee, can help elucidate a process whose odds, more often than not, can feel insurmountable:

1. Connections: Since the best way to get an agent's attention is to be referred by someone they know, get to know someone they know. This means rolling up your sleeves and playing "Six Degrees Of Fill-In-Agent's-Name-Here." Any friend of a neighbor of a relative will do, just as long as you're not overtly mercenary about your reasons for contacting them. And even if you are, it never hurts to ask. An agent is far more likely to respond to a message whose subject line reads: "Calling at the suggestion of so-and-so" than they are to one in which a script is being (self)-proclaimed as the next *Sixth Sense*.

2. Once you have them on the phone: Remember that they don't really want to hear much about you as a person; to paraphrase Sir Laurence Olivier, they can fake their sincere concern later on. The best approach is to introduce yourself, remind the agent about your connection to him, then pitch your script as succinctly as possible. If it's a high-concept or provocative script, this should be the easy part: give them the hook, then sum it up with the *Blank* meets *Blank* approach that was discussed earlier. If you haven't written something so obviously commercial you should describe it with as much passion as possible while keeping it brief, and still wrapping it up with the *Blank* meets *Blank* equation.

3. If you have to pitch yourself: This falls squarely into the Plan B category – as the agent interviewed below can confirm, they sign people mostly on the basis of referrals. Still, it is not unheard of to get representation off a blind query letter; try anything you can to forge a personal connection (e.g. "I understand you're a big Bruin basketball fan; do you think Coach Howland is making as much progress as he should have by this point?"), then go through the steps outlined above.

The good news with query letter that you can afford to describe your project with a bit more detail than that permitted by the phone; most agents will gladly read a paragraph in lieu of listening to an unseasoned writer's verbosity, plus you get the added advantage of constructed sentences over impromptu conversation – always a plus for someone trained in the art of the written word. The bad news is that most blind queries wind up in the garbage can, unread. And remember, do not send a script until the agent officially gives you the green light – some agencies will even send a disclosure form for you to fill out to avoid any confusion. Make sure that agent personally requests the script, as opposed to the assistant who "thinks their boss wants to read it"; assistants don't have that level of authority even though, as the next section will discuss, they can be tremendously helpful to you.

4. How many agencies should you submit to? As many as possible; you are under no obligation to wait for an official pass before exposing the script to other agents. Though you never want an agent playing the numbers game with you, it is not a bad idea to do it on your end given the long odds involved.

5. Once a few weeks have gone by: Start following up. Get to know the names of the agents' assistants and always be nice, regardless of how snottily they treat you. Remember that they talk to dozens of you a week; as far as they're concerned, you're no different from a pesky telemarketer who calls repeatedly during dinner. And should you get the feeling that you're dealing with an actual human being instead of a headset with a suit he can't really afford, try anything you can to make a connection; you would be surprised at how many assistants stayed on their boss to return a phone call, all because they liked the voice of the person on the other end. Should you and an assistant get along based on your common likes and dislikes (hint: everyone in the film business – especially an employee as underpaid as an assistant – loves movies), ask them how long they've been working there. In most cases, assistants are trainees who are on track for promotion to junior agent status, which means that if you can, try to suss out how far away that date might be and work the relationship; believe it or not, it is not at all uncommon for a successful writer/agent collaboration to begin in this fashion.

6. How often to call: Every other week following the initial three-week grace period. You want to be consistent, yet not too persistent; checking in, as opposed to reminding. Also, despite the butterflies swarming your stomach at the prospect of real industry feedback, be patient; you will earn bonus points for being well-aware of the staggering amount of material an agent must read in any given week.

Remember, too, that their existing clients will always come first. Don't try to goose the process with transparent bluff tactics ("I'm getting great feedback from CAA"), or with irrelevant information ("So-and-so's head of development is reading it as we speak"). On the other hand, if you do have positive response from a competing agency – or from someone at a production company or studio – make sure to convey this fact to the assistant, or to the agent directly, provided she is taking your call. Do this especially if you're close to an offer from another agency; it's considered bad protocol to give someone a window of opportunity to consider you, then take it away without at least giving them due notice.

7. Learn when to throw in the towel: Contrary to the way it works in movies, persistence doesn't always pay off; if a few months have gone by without any response, and you've left four or five messages, then it's time to move on.

8. If you are lucky enough to have your choice of agents: After a hearty pat on the back and an acknowledgment that this dilemma falls squarely into the "embarrassment of riches" department, there is still a big decision to be made.

After meeting with the interested parties, ask yourself the following questions: who sounds more passionate about my work? Who seems to have a plan of action and a clear vision for my career? Who seems to be more honest about my chances? (Believe it or not, there are still plenty of decent, honest agents out there; a good agent should be able to level with you not only about your possibilities in the marketplace, but also about the quality of your work.) And which agency felt like a better fit for you, not only professionally but personally as well? This question will be addressed further in the next section.

Majors and Boutiques

Agencies in the entertainment industry tend to fall into two categories: majors and boutiques. The majors are also known as the Big Five and are the biggest outfits in town due to their mix of actors, directors, and writers. They include the following: Creative Artist's Agency (CAA), International Creative Management (ICM), The William Morris Agency (WMA or William Morris), United Talent Agency (UTA), and Endeavor. Paradigm, a former boutique, is en route to becoming a major after merging with two other well-regarded boutiques. The boutique agencies include places like the Gersh Agency and the Agency for Performing Arts (APA), who tend to represent writers and directors only (although the consolidation atmosphere of the corporate world is very much alive in the agency business as well and several of these boutiques are evaluating their viability without a strong actor clientele).

The general consensus is that boutiques provide the writer with a more personal touch, especially one who is just getting going, because they aren't as busy catering to their big ticket items (the movie stars and A-list directors). While there is some truth to this, it is also important to remember that your agent will be your point person in all your business dealings. Thus it is really the agent who will determine just how much attention you will receive. There are writers at majors who haven't yet earned the agency a ton of money but speak with their agent twice or three times a week (in most cases, this will be an agent who has just started out and is a bit hungrier) while other writers at boutiques can barely get their agent on the phone. So the industry adage that "it's not the agency, it's the agent" is true and thus requires you to really know who you're doing business with.

But what are the basic advantages of being with a major versus the advantages of being at a boutique? There is certainly the attention factor; agents at majors are competing with other agents within their agency to get writers assignments, which essentially means that you are competing with many of the agency's other writers for jobs. Since boutiques have fewer clients, there is not as much competition within their walls. But should you get the impression that an agent at a major is the right choice, consider that he or she has access to the kind of talent that can turn a cold script into a hot script overnight with a simple "yes." This is a process known as "packaging" and although it happens with far less frequency than agents would have you believe, it is nonetheless possible. Another lesser-known factor in making this decision is that when studios make writing assignments available, the big five are often the only agencies whom they actively solicit for writers; the boutiques have to cover the studios harder and fight harder for their clients, which is eminently possible but does requires that an agent put in extra hustle time in order to nail down the gigs for their clients.

So how should you make your decision? For starters, if you are lucky enough to know any studio executives or producers ask them which agents fight the hardest for their clients (which they always know and are usually happy to pass on). Is the agent in question a tough negotiator, or does he sometimes cross the line and talk his clients out of deals? Is he well-regarded around town or has he burned too many people? How strong are his relationships with the young executives and up-and-coming producers who will be hungrier for new material than people higher up on the food chain? If you don't know an industry insider who can give you the basic scoop, try to get as many of these answers as possible when you actually do meet with the agent for the first time. Remember that this could be one of the most important decisions you ever make in your career, and your excitement at being in the room, surrounded by people in expensive suits, should in no way mitigate your need to know as much as possible about the person with whom you are about to do business.

Joe vs. the Volcano

How Joe Ezsterhas Took on Mike Ovitz's Foot Soldiers and Won

In the late 1980's, there was no writer in Hollywood hotter than Joe Ezsterhas. A former Rolling Stone writer who then went on to pen the films *Flashdance* and *Jagged Edge*, he had an enviable track record. He also happened to be a prolific writer of spec scripts and believed that writing without a studio executive looking over your shoulder was the only way to preserve a writer's vision. In 1986 a five month Writer's Guild strike stopped the flow of scripts into the studios completely, and when the strike ended the studios were desperate to buy new material for their now-dry development slates. No one had hotter material than Ezsterhas, and he soon began receiving staggering fees for his spec work, becoming perhaps the first-ever "brand name" screenwriter. Ezsterhas' sale of *Basic Instinct* for four million dollars set a record, but the film went on to earn hundreds of millions worldwide and cemented Ezsterhas' reputation as a bankable commercial commodity. He was represented by CAA, at the time the most powerful agency in Hollywood thanks to its founder Michael Ovitz, and Ezsterhas was one of the few writers whom Ovitz represented personally.

Trouble began when Ezsterhas' former agent Guy McIllwayne, who years ago had left the agency business to become a producer, returned to ICM. Ezsterhas had enjoyed an exceptionally close relationship with McIllwayne that was akin to a mentorship, and while he was in no way being done a disservice by his association with CAA and Ovitz he missed the personal touch that McIllwayne had provided for years. Ezsterhas informed Ovitz that he intended to leave CAA in favor of McIllwayne, that it was in no way a reflection of his feelings for the agency's service but rather due to a more personal element.

Ovitz, however, took it personally. A lifelong acolyte of the manifesto *The Art Of War*, he understood that power has as much to do with perception as anything; if his agency couldn't keep the hottest writer in town in its fold, it would be a major chink in their otherwise impervious armor. As Ezsterhas tells the story (Ovitz, of course, has a far different recollection), Ovitz called Ezsterhas into his office and, without breaking his smile, informed Ezsterhas that he wouldn't be leaving. Period. A reference was made to his foot soldiers (CAA famously had a group of twentysomething agents referred to as the *Young Turks*) whom Ovitz claimed would lay waste to Ezsterhas' career. Ezsterhas left the office feeling helpless, and for good reason; that year, *Premiere* magazine had ranked Ovitz number one on its Hollywood power list... for the third year in a row.

At a loss, Ezsterhas went back to his roots. He was used to receiving press for his spec sales, but he'd now need something far bigger than a fluff piece that bragged about his riches. He wrote Ovitz a long, angry letter, referenced Ovitz's threats specifically and told him that he was leaving (but not without a hearty, four-letter salute), then "leaked" the Ovitz letter to a source at the local paper. Within hours, the Ezsterhas story was the hottest news item in Hollywood, and Ovitz had no choice but to shrug and distance himself from the unhappy scribe, and Ezsterhas, for his part, got to prove that the pen is, indeed, mightier than the Armani suit.

Smaller Agents

Let's return once again to the film *Jerry Maguire*, in which Tom Cruise's eponymous character goes through a crisis of conscience and decides to head out on his own to service clients in a decent and ethical way. Okay, nice movie; now are there any real-life equivalents? The good news is, yes; plenty of agents find that the politics of any big agency – and some boutiques are big enough so that politics become a factor – are simply not what they had in mind when they decided to enter the field. And because hanging one's own shingle, complete with rented office space and paid assistant, involves overhead that is coming out of one's own pocket, the pressure to land jobs for clients and earn commission is far greater than it ever used to be.

This can be extremely good news for the overlooked-but-talented writer who simply needs more hand holding and direction than any major or decent-sized boutique is willing or able to offer. You will face virtually no interior competition and enjoy far more access to an agent with his or her own outfit (or one that features a partnership between two or three agents). The only drawback is that they had better be working their studio and producer relationships tirelessly because none of the major players in town in charge of hiring writers will actively be soliciting smaller agents for their clients' services.

Signing With an Agent

Once you have officially been accepted into the agency and have been taken out once or twice for drinks or dinner to celebrate, you'll be given a stack of papers to sign – not to worry, nearly all agencies use a boilerplate agreement that stipulates that they represent your work and are entitled to ten percent of anything they sell and negotiate. Before you panic and start calling a lawyer to go through the thing with a fine-tooth comb, remember this: any agency contract can be nullified if the agent has not gotten you work in ninety days.

Also remember that no agency wants to keep an unhappy client, because it creates more problems for them. If you aren't clicking with your agent and think you have options elsewhere, move on; no one takes it personally, and the game of agency musical chairs that clients play is done with such regularity that it can appear almost comical at times. Plus, these contracts, regardless of the agency in question, are strictly boilerplate, and are in no way written to swindle you out of your hard-earned money.

Agent agendas

Even though the agent/writer relationship is structured so as to be incentive-based, agents can still have agendas that are not in a writer's best interest. As discussed, there will be times when two writers in an agency might be competing for the same writing assignment without knowing it; as unfortunate a reality as this is, even worse is the reality of agencies "prioritizing" their clients and deciding who will and will not be exposed to studios for various gigs. Unfortunately, it is next to impossible for a writer to know exactly what goes on behind agency doors, so all you have to rely upon is what your agent tells you.

Still, there are agendas that are clearer. When it comes time to send out your spec script, you should have an excellent idea of which producers would be right for the project (a more detailed analysis of the spec script process will follow later). Sometimes your agent will sidestep a producer you have in mind, explaining that "so and so" is really looking for something like this. But after doing some research on the producer they have in mind and going through their list of credits, you can't figure out what he or she would add to the script's vitality. Which then leads you to one, or several, of the following conclusions:

1. The agent is a close friend of the producer's and is trying to throw the producer a bone.

2. The agent owes the producer a favor and is using your script to call in a chip.

3. The agent is actually sleeping with the producer.

While none of these motivations are unethical in the true sense of the word, every one is unacceptable in its own way. You need to remember that, as disempowered as writers can be made to feel at times, your hard work is not a pawn in the agent's game and he needs to do the right thing by your script. Which means that if you have to put your foot down and inform your agent that you would simply rather go to a different producer, then that is your prerogative.

Q&A: Hollywood Agent at Paradigm

An agent at Paradigm, a leading talent and literary agency, had the following advice to offer:

What is a typical day for you?

Typical day means getting in by 9 a.m. and, two to three days a week, going to morning meetings. I read my new e-mails as soon as I can and respond to any e-mails I have from the night before. After that, really every day is different. Most afternoons are full of clients coming up to meet, or going on studio rounds. Most of our business is done over the phone, so we spend a lot of time calling studio execs and production execs to put clients up for jobs and find out what their needs are. At the end of the day, I return the calls that I missed throughout the day. I usually have a screening or something to do three nights a week. I guess simply put, 60% of my day is spent on the phone, 20% speaking with colleagues in meetings and 20% reading, watching reels, replying to emails.

What can a writer do to get your attention?

Really for a new writer to get in front of an agent, they need to have a connection to the agency somehow. Either a manager needs to refer them, or they have to know an assistant, or a lawyer or a friend of an agent's etc. It is incredibly rare that a writer will write a query letter that gets him an agent. If the writer has no connections to agents, then I would suggest competitions. Most agencies will read the Nicholls finalists and other programs' winners. Also, try to get in front of a young manager. These guys read voraciously and when they are not reading, they are making introductions to agents for themselves and their clients.

What advice would you give to writers who are just getting started?

Write something commercial. The hardest thing to do is write a beautiful little story that you have always wanted to write that can be made for a million bucks. It might show someone you have a great voice, but at the end of the day, the way to get introduced to the town is a spec sale. Also, the way to get a team of representation around you is to give them a piece of commercial material they feel they can sell.

How can a writer best keep the lines of communication open between himself and his representation?

Once you have representation a good agent should be talking to you all the time. Agents hate to call just to check in (or at least I do), I feel like it is pointless if there is nothing to talk about. If I was a writer and I wasn't getting any attention from an agent, it means two things.

1. You as the writer are not doing enough. You need to be coming up with ideas, chasing down rights, writing a spec etc. Of course this is only true if you are not working consistently as a writer.

2. If you are working steadily and you are still not hearing regularly from your agent, you probably need a new agent.

Anything else a budding screenwriter should know?

Be tenacious. Learn how to pitch your writing. I have been to countless pitch fests and spoken at a ton of seminars and the people whose material I will read are the people I like. The people who can pitch their material and make me want to read it. Have a great one liner for your material. Also, before you give a script to a potential agent/manager/lawyer, everyone you know better have read it. Your mom, aunt, mailman, and local cop should have all read it. I hate getting scripts that I feel like are fresh off the printer and no one has truly sat down with to look it over. I never put down a script because I feel like someone put months into it; however, if a writer gives me a script full of typos and mistakes, I'll put it down without hesitation. I think that's it. The most important thing for a young writer to know is that a good script will always find its way into the hands of someone who can do something with it.

Managers, Attorneys, and the Writer's Guild

CHAPTER 9

Beyond the necessary evil (as it were) that is an agent, there is an additional layer of service providers known as managers and attorneys. Managers and attorneys both fall into the same category of optional service providers; neither is absolutely necessary, but there are upsides to hiring both. The downside, of course, is extra commission out of your pocket, and in every case you have to assess whether or not you feel these people are worth the money they are costing you.

While a combination of both alongside an agent can be a formidable negotiating team, one that sometimes justifies the extra commission you are paying out, you never want to find yourself stuck in a position where you are carrying around "dead weight" – representatives who are earning commission off of you but aren't contributing much toward your bottom line or your career development. Make sure that, even if the manager wasn't the one to get you your last assignment, that he is at least putting you up for new ones (or at very least are trying to generate work for you in some other arena). It's hard to make a case, so to speak, against the conventional wisdom of having a lawyer look over your contracts, but should you be paying commission or hourly? The following sections should help make sense of the process that – embarrassment of riches though it may seem – is nonetheless a complicated one for a writer.

Managers

In the past several years, the entertainment industry has seen an increase in managerial companies that open their doors to writers. Which begs the question: what could a manager possibly offer a writer? After all, aren't they more for ill-tempered movie stars who are unhappy with the size of their trailers and the colors of the M&Ms in their hospitality suite? The answer, of course, is that used in conjunction with an agent, a manager can be a potent tool for a writer, especially to one who is just starting out.

What does a manager do?

Contrary to outside perception, a manager is more than someone who simpl
strokes your ego when the industry doesn't respond to your work. Their

is, as their title would indicate, to manage your career: offer concrete career guidance, help you navigate the tricky and unpredictable turns projects can take, and intervene on your behalf whenever necessary. They also offer script notes and counsel you on which ideas of yours they feel have real commercial possibilities. And the bigger outfits have high-end directors and actors who heed the advice of their managers, often more than they would that of their agents, which means that you as a writer have a pipeline to the kind of talent that can change your script's fortune.

Managers, with the exception of the ones who work at the bigger companies, are often far more accessible than agents and can often serve as a conduit to getting you read by an agent which, at the end of the day, is still a writer's primary representative and the only one that is truly indispensable. And in the likely event that your agent finds himself too busy to take and return your phone calls should you be experiencing a cold spell (expect it – it's one of the unfortunate realities of the business), a manager should provide the more personal touch and be the person to whom you should turn to stoke the embers of your career and strategize to turn things around.

What's the difference between an agent and a manager?

In some ways, managers function very much like agents. They work solely on commission and command 10 percent of your salary in exchange for their services; they go to studios and do everything in their power to hustle up work for their clients; and when a spec script is being prepared to send out on the marketplace, a manager will frequently make as many phone calls as an agent.

Although your manager is ostensibly the more personal connection of the two, there are managers who function more like agents and agents who function more like managers in this department. Like agencies, management companies can be large or small, although the difference in size tends to be more extreme and most managers who service writers tend to be independent entities on the order of former agents who, armed with a few of their most loyal clients, are now striking out on their own.

[illegible]ere is, however, one critical difference between the two: a manager is [illegible]ted to produce projects. Sometimes this pertains to projects that are not [illegible]ed by their clients, but more often than not it is their own clients [illegible]roject they are producing. Before you cry "foul," however, it is [illegible] to note that managers are not allowed to "double dip" on the financial end: they can either manage the client's project as a commissioned party, or they can opt to produce and receive a fee when – or if – the project gets made. Still, there are those in the industry who feel that a manager who can produce a client's work presents a sticky conflict of interest: say, for example, a writer is about to be removed from a project by the studio. The manager who is acting as producer on the project now must go along with the firing of his or her client, since the studio in the end controls the purse strings. Naturally, the writer would feel some degree of resentment while continuing to work on future projects with the manager. Even in less clear-cut cases, writers need to think long and hard before agreeing to let their manager produce a project. Producing requires a different set of skills than managing does, and managers who thrive on the immediacy of setting up projects and of addressing tasks at hand frequently lack the producer's eye for seeing possibilities that are not yet on the table.

Other professional considerations

It is important to keep in mind that many agents view the hiring of a manager as an indirect accusation that they aren't doing their job. Managers fire back that if agents were, in fact, doing their job, then why has there been such a dramatic increase in managerial shingles offering services to writers? In the worst possible case scenario, the writer feels like the child in a divorce: caught between two warring parties whose ostensible purpose it is to be nurturing him or her. The truth is that managers have something to offer in conjunction with agents, and that if all parties can be convinced of the benefits of working together (which, more often than not they can), the benefits yielded by everyone involved will be exponential.

Also, you need to make sure that you don't wind up in a situation where the right hand has no idea what the left hand is doing. The communication level – or lack thereof – between agents and managers can be downright awful and more than one writer has complained that, for all the commission they're shelling out (managers and agents each earn ten percent of a writer's income), they're simply not being serviced.

Entertainment Attorneys

Like any other business, the entertainment business has contracts that can be reams of pages long. And even though it is technically the job of your agent to negotiate the terms of this contract, good business wisdom dictates that you should never sign a contract without first having it looked at by an attorney.

Wiser yet, you should make sure the attorney in question specializes in entertainment law. And, unlike typical attorneys, most entertainment attorneys work on commission in the same way as managers and agents (although, unlike managers and agents, attorneys typically take five percent of their clients' earnings). Attorneys can also be instrumental in creating relationships between their clients, although you shouldn't necessarily expect this from them as this tends to be more the responsibility of your agent.

A good entertainment attorney will be familiar with the practices employed by the studios, will be familiar with the studios' business affairs people (the lawyers employed by the studios to negotiate on the studio's behalf), and will negotiate, in conjunction with your agent, the terms of a sale. He or she will also understand the role of a producer and will be aware of what is standard and not standard with regard to how much work you should or should not be doing (a detailed description of what is encompassed in a typical studio assignment will be covered in greater detail in our studio overview).

A good entertainment attorney should examine every angle and possibility of the intellectual property (in this case, your script) they represent and include these considerations in the contract. Say, for example, your script is ultimately spun off into a television show. Even though that show's principals are based on characters you created, in most cases an outside writer who is more familiar with the television format will be brought in to create a pilot. The question is then what degree of ownership of the show should you be granted? What about merchandising (toys and other such movie-related items) should your script turn into the next *Finding Nemo*? While all monies directly pertaining to the film's success will be determined by stipulations set forth by the Writer's Guild (see below), there are ramifications that go well beyond your script and its immediate, pertinent duties, as the example below will show.

Case Study

Steven Brill and The Mighty Ducks

In the early 1990s, a screenwriter named Steven Brill, who'd sold a few scripts, sold one to Walt Disney Pictures called *The Mighty Ducks*. A fan of the underdog sports classic *The Bad News Bears*, Brill envisioned a similar model, only set against the backdrop of the burgeoning world of hockey. Michael Eisner, the chairman of the Disney company who had hockey-playing sons, was excited over the idea of making a youth-themed hockey movie and committed to making the picture, which not only went on to become one of the bigger hits of 1994 but also spawned two sequels. Brill's career took off, and he soon found himself in the company of the industry's highest-paid comedy writers.

He also found himself somewhere else – namely a series of civil courts. For Disney, eager to expand its empire, had decided to venture into the world of sports. Their first venture was to buy a hockey team and name it... The Mighty Ducks. The Mighty Ducks played in Anaheim and soon became a major draw, as did their distinctive, duck-billed merchandising. Everyone in the Disney empire was thrilled with their success; everyone except Steven Brill, who felt that the name he had come up with and the film he had written had been a major part of the multi-million dollar franchise. Brill sued Disney for a proprietary piece of the Mighty Ducks, and was ultimately awarded an undisclosed sum of money, but not before having done battle with Disney for years.

On the flip side, when George Lucas was finalizing his deal with Twentieth Century Fox over *Star Wars*, his lawyers and Fox's were stuck on one deal point. "Let them have it," Lucas instructed his lawyers. "Just give me total control of merchandising." Fox's executives did some research and discovered that the entire studio had banked a little over a million dollars in merchandising the year before. They gave it to him... and one very costly mistake later helped usher in a new era in Hollywood.

The Writer's Guild

The Writer's Guild is the union that acts on the behalf of writers with regard to the studios, the same way any other union negotiates on behalf of its members. It is divided into two branches – Writer's Guild of America West (WGAW) and Writer's Guild of America East (WGAE). In addition to negotiating the collective bargaining agreement between its members and the studios, the Guild – in exchange for one-and-a-quarter percent of its members' dues, provides its members with several other valuable services that are listed below.

1. Residuals: Residuals are the royalties paid to members of the Guild by the studios whenever a writer's film is played on television (either domestically or overseas), is rented in a video store, is purchased on DVD, or earns any other form of ancillary income for the studio that produced it. The studios compute the writer's residuals based on scales agreed to by the Guild and the studios, then sends a check to the Guild which is then forwarded to the writer. The checks, which until recently were issued in green envelopes that earned them the nickname "greenies," are like found money, especially for writers going through a dry spell who open their mailbox one day to find a few thousand dollars waiting for them. Residuals were a hard-fought battle that had to be fought (decades ago, writers earned no such income, although pre-television and home video it wasn't much of an issue) and are still being fought; the Guild recently averted a strike where the issues at stake, among others, were revenue from new revenue streams like Internet and DVDs (the former hasn't presented itself as much of an issue and the latter, unfortunately, didn't yield much of a budge from the studios). In addition to providing an indispensable service, the Guild's residuals department is easily accessible and the people who work there are invariably responsive and efficient in helping writers track down residuals that may have experienced a delay (which happens from time to time) or in letting writers know when they can expect a check in the near future. The Guild tracks residuals and includes them in your dues statements for you so that you don't have to compute them yourself when it comes time to figure out your quarterly dues.

2. Health care: One of the Guild's most famous perks – deservedly so – is its health insurance plan. If you earn a certain amount of money per year, you qualify for the Guild's health plan. Of course, you have to maintain that level of income every year, but if you earn past a certain amount, you receive bonus points that can be redeemed during dry spells. And the plan itself is without peer; writers enjoy among the widest range of health professionals and close to the highest rate of compensation in the country (indeed, it is not unreasonable to expect that even a high-risk pregnancy will wind up costing the writer under whose plan the gestation is covered practically nothing). In the past, the plan had been free year-round, but the Guild has unfortunately had to make adjustments given the skyrocketing costs of health care; members are now charged a quarterly fee that, while not cheap, still pales in comparison to the scope of services they are provided.

3. Pension: The Writer's Guild is also in charge of making sure that a certain amount of a writer's earnings from any particular studio are contributed to the writer's pension plan. Like most pensions, there are qualifications and stipulations that mandate how long and to what degree a writer must have worked in order to cash in on his or her pension, but as with the other services the Guild provides, there is a comprehensive booklet that explains eligibility and payout.

4. Arbitration: Whenever you see the words "written by" during the opening credits of a movie followed by several names, chances are that several writers were employed at various times during the production. So who should get credit? This is where the Guild steps in; on any film that employed more than one writer (or one writing team), the Guild will automatically send it to arbitration. What this entails is the Guild making copies of every draft of the script, then removing the writers' names from the cover (so as to ensure objectivity) and sending them to a three-person committee that has been assembled for the express purpose of determining credits for this particular film. The committee then, based on predetermined guidelines, reads the drafts and tries to determine who has made enough contributions to the story, characters, and dialogue so as to warrant screen credit.

This is more than an issue of mere pride; back-end residuals are paid out only to the writers who receive screen credit, which frequently translates into thousands of dollars. Often you will see "story by writer A" and "screenplay by writer B," which means that the committee felt that writer A deserved some credit for coming up with the idea for the story as well as some of its developments, but that the actual characters and dialogue were more or less the contributions of writer B. Or you'll see "written by writer A and writer B." This is different than "written by writer A & writer B" because the word "and" connotes two different writers, whereas an ampersand (&) signifies a writing team.

5. Writer's Guild Magazine and Newsletter: The magazine *Written By*, is the official monthly periodical of the Writer's Guild that is sent to members free of charge (non-members can subscribe or, if they live near an eclectic newsstand, can purchase a copy). In addition to profiles of successful writers, *Written By* features monthly columns that tackle everything from career advice to the writer's fragile mental state and how best to cope with it. *The Writer's Guild Newsletter* (which is also sent out electronically to members) informs member of upcoming Guild-sponsored events like free screenings, topic discussion panels, softball games, and niche writers' get-togethers.

Contact information: The Guild's main telephone number is (323) 782-4700, or you can log onto its website at www.wga.org.

Producers and Studios

CHAPTER 10

Now that you have put the issue of your representation to bed, it is time to "go out" with your script and try to sell it. The first step your agent (and manager, if you have one) will take is to draw up a list of producers to whom they wish to show the script. However, this is not the money part of the equation, but rather another step in the sales process. The key difference between producers and studios is that for the most part, producers are the salespeople who try to push your script through the studio, which acts as the buyer.

Producers

Art Linson, the producer of such hit films as *Fast Times At Ridgemont High* and, more recently, *Seven*, once famously quipped, "A producer is a dog with a script in its mouth." This quote is every bit as elucidating as it is entertaining, for in one simple line it establishes the producer's position in Hollywood – always a "yes" or a "no" away from glory or failure.

A true producer – as opposed to the multitude of executive producers, associate producers, and co-producers whose names litter the opening credits of any given film these days – does everything from get the script sold to (or "set up at") a studio to developing it with the writer – or, more likely, writers – involved. A producer will then be instrumental in attracting talent that will get the film made (stars and directors) and using that talent to leverage the studio into "green-lighting" (committing to fund) the movie. The producer will be on the set, serving as a liaison between the director and the studio, especially if the two are at odds on either creative or budgetary issues.

It is up to the producer to see to it that the production runs as smoothly as possible, and that the same is true for the post-production (editing, reshoots, sound mixing, etc.). They fight for optimum release dates – preferably not the same weekend as DreamWorks' latest *Shrek* installment – and then cross their fingers and hope for the kind of opening weekend that will ensure a hit, or at least for good enough word of mouth that will ensure, if not the kind of box office numbers that make studio executives drool, at least a decent performance on DVD. This process takes anywhere from two to five years (*Forrest Gump* famously took twelve). That is, if it happens at all.

Why do you need to know all this? Because there is one thing conspicuously absent from the above list of duties: namely, the power to purchase a script.

A producer is, at the end of the day, a more powerful seller than you. A producer may have a deal with a studio in which the studio covers the producer's office expenses and overhead in exchange for a first look at all his projects, or he might have an exclusive deal that stipulates that he is not permitted to produce projects for any other studio. A producer may even have something known as a "discretionary fund," which permits him to option scripts for a lower amount of money (in most cases) than a studio would have paid, so that the producer can further develop the script. But a producer cannot essentially buy a script. This is an important distinction that you need to know; many writers, upon first starting out, are mistakenly under the impression that a good meeting with a producer means they've got a sale under their belt, which couldn't be farther from the truth.

Producers are the first step in getting a script set up; when it is time for your agent to send out your script, the producers are the first stop. Which means that your agent will draw up a list of producers whom she feels will respond to the material, then send the script to them in the hopes that they can set it up at either the studio with whom they have a deal, or at another studio with whom they have a good relationship. Studios tend to look to certain producers to make certain kinds of films for them, and if your script does happen to fall into that category then it helps to have a producer attached who has a track record.

A producer can also be a helpful tool in developing a script from the ground up. If you have found a producer with whom you feel a decent connection and who produces the kinds of films you are interested in writing, take a meeting and pitch him some ideas. Chances are, he might be able to bring up some red flags – either commercially or creatively – that you might not have considered. And if the two of you should happen to find an idea that you'd like to develop together, then the producer can serve as a sounding board and rudder to help you write the script. Because the creative process can be so lonely and because at times you'll feel like you're writing in a vacuum without any input, working with a producer from the ground up can be extremely helpful. In the best possible scenario, the producer will function as a combination of writing partner and editor; sometimes producers and writers even share story credit on a project, but only if producers either suggested the story or worked on it so much that it is warranted.

While it is customary for a writer to do a free pass for a producer prior to turning the draft into the studio, there are producers who abuse this right and ask for draft after draft with the implicit "you'll never work in this town again" threat underlying their bullying. Unless the producer in question is one of the two or three biggest names in town (and if he is, you should do everything in your power to please him), you should have your agent stand up for you and demand that the draft be turned in to the studio. For starters, you can't get paid for your work until you do so; a producer who is demanding such extensive rewrites is essentially making you work for free and denying you your right to get paid. In addition, the studio executives might very well be getting annoyed by the delay in the draft, and because these people are the buyers who are signing your checks it is in your best interests to remain on their good sides.

Tips From a Producer

- It's true that you should write what you know, but unfortunately high-concept movies tend to be out-there premises that don't feel terribly personal. The difference between the ones that truly resonate with us and the ones that don't are that in the ones we move forward with, the writer has cleverly figured out a way to infuse his or her worldview or something universal or something really personal into the characters and their situations.
- That said, I love nothing more than to discover a great voice or sensibility. It took Charlie Kaufman a long time to sell his scripts, but even the people who passed on him initially thought that he had something terrific to say. There's nothing wrong with writing what you think you can sell, but I read hundreds of generic scripts like that. Commerciality can't come completely at the expense of your original voice.
- As a producer, I function as the gateway to the studio. Make good use of me; use me as a sounding board to better understand the studio's sensibilities, which change from week to week, usually depending on what's number one at the box office.
- Feel free to kick some ideas around. I've helped scores of writers sell spec scripts and can save you a lot of time and despair in chasing a concept down a path that has absolutely no chance of selling. And only the sleaziest producers in the business steal ideas; your agent should have a pretty good idea who has a good reputation and who doesn't.
- Most of the time you'll be dealing with my development executives. Don't interpret this as a sign of disinterest on my part; working with writers is why they're here. More often than not I'm off in meetings trying to get talent attached to my projects that haven't been green-lit, or away on the set of my projects that have.

Studios

As the buyer in the equation, the studio is inevitably the last stop on your script's tour. Once your script is submitted to the studio, you will feel as though your fate is in God's hands. Because it isn't enough to simply have written a good script; it has to fit a specific business need the studio has, and be well-timed to boot. Say a supernatural horror film came out on Friday, and by Monday it was number one at the box office. That morning the studio has its staff meeting to go over projects, and everyone decides that they need a supernatural horror script. On Tuesday, your agent sends out your script, which happens to be a high-concept, well-written, supernatural horror film. Your script has a fairly good chance of being purchased.

On the other hand, let's say that your script goes out the same time as 10 other scripts that fit the bill… and one of them is being pushed by the studio's favorite producer in this genre, or by a producer to whom the production head happens to owe a favor, or by the production company or a movie star with whom the studio desperately wants to be in business, and they'll make this a two-for-one deal… the possibilities go on and on. As do the "close, but no cigar" possibilities; say you happen to send out your script a few weeks later, but every studio in town already has their supernatural horror script and is loath to buy another. Chances are that you will not sell your script because the windows of opportunity open and close very quickly in the studio buying game.

Which is not to say that everything is based on timing; certain genres (like romantic comedy) never go out of style. Nor does a script that is either undeniably well-written or brilliantly conceived-M. Night Shyamalan could probably have sold *The Sixth Sense* under any circumstances. The same holds true for Josh Goldsmith and Cathy Yuspa, who fleshed-out what is one of the best high-concept pitches of all time in *What Women Want* – the premise was so universally appealing that it didn't matter if the script was somewhat lacking (which it was).

So who are these people who decide your fate on the studio level? There are several rungs in the chain of command, but only a few who have the actual power to say "yes" and render a financial decision. So, from the ground up, this is your basic studio power hierarchy:

Story editor

Story editors are primarily readers for studios who take part in studio meetings. Though they frequently attend staff meetings, their job is primarily to cover the bushels of scripts that are submitted to the studio. Though their hours are long (late into the night and through the weekend more often than not), these are plum positions for young people trying to angle their way into the industry; story editors can be promoted in good time, thanks to the high turnover rate of the studio executive ranks.

Creative executive

A creative executive, or "C.E.," is the junior executive on any given project. Although they are full-fledged studio executives, they are inevitably paired up with a more senior executive (usually a vice president) on any given project. A creative executive's job is to be the studio's first official "read," once a script has been favorably covered. The C.E. then either brings the script up for discussion at staff meetings or, if the script is on a tight deadline and might sell sooner than that, will pass it along to a vice president in order to drum up some senior support to buy it. Creative executives also meet with prospective writers for assignments and rewrites, as well as with writers on projects that are in active development, and it is usually the job of the C.E. to type up notes from the meetings and send them to the vice president so that the project's creative direction can be tracked.

Director of development

A director of development is a slightly better-paid version of a C.E., and it is a position that not all studios use. Directors of development can often individually champion a project, but there will almost always need to be a vice president overseeing it.

Vice presidents

There are three classifications of vice president in a studio: vice president, senior vice president, and executive vice president (in ascending order). Being promoted to vice president – usually based on your savvy for picking commercial properties, ability to get along with the upper echelons of the power ranks, or a combination of both – is an executive's first taste of real power; in addition to receiving perks such as expense accounts and car leases, vice presidents oversee a plethora of projects in various stages of development. And even though they do not technically have the power to buy a script, they can often fight hard to make a significant difference in a script's fate. They are also the last line of creative development; once they are through giving notes, the script is now placed on the consideration block – green-lit projects (or flashing yellows, which means that they're going to move forward contingent upon talent attachments or budget approval) bode well for a vice president, but turnaround (which means that the studio has decided to drop the project) does not. Vice presidents are also often shuttled to and from various movie sets to oversee the production; this can entail such inglorious duties as firing a director or dealing with a petulant star's unreasonable requests, but mostly they are there to check up on the status of the film and make sure everything is running smoothly.

President of production

The president of production is in charge of acquiring and overseeing the studio's entire development slate. The president is the only staff member who can officially purchase a spec script, and frequently must approve of writers for assignments and rewrites as well (although this is not always the case and depends on the executives on the project as well as the project itself – clearly the writers approved to rewrite *Spider Man 2* would warrant far greater scrutiny than those assigned to take on *Because of Winn Dixie*). The president manages the staff and helps determine the course of the studio's development direction (e.g. more horror, more comedy, less big-budget action) and presents the development slate for the approval of the studio's chairman. The president is often called upon to work with a project's producer in the ongoing attempt to woo the town's movie stars and directors that will make that project all the more palatable to the chairman.

Chairman of the studio

The chairman is in charge of the studio's film production. The chairman (or woman, as is often the case) is presented a list of projects for consideration by the president and must decide which of those films the studio is willing to green-light and at what budget. The chairman reports directly to the studio's CEO and, given the ever-expanding nature of entertainment empires, might be called upon to synergize the studio's slate of films with the various merchandising or theme park interests held by the studio's parent company. The chairman of the studio is one of the most powerful people in town; virtually all of them are listed in high positions on *Premiere* magazine's Power 100 (which is the entertainment industry's gold standard of power).

A Week in the Life of a Spec Script

Monday

- Meet with agent and manager to draw up submission list.
- Settle on producers whom everyone feels will respond to the script.
- Sneak the script to one or two "guaranteed" good reads who will hopefully get the ball rolling quickly.
- Take prescribed dose of Ambien to calm the butterflies and get to sleep.

Tuesday

- Script officially "goes out" – agents and managers call the producers on their list, who either arrange to pick up a hard copy of the script or have it e-mailed to them.
- Both reads come in from the night before; one is passing – liked the writing, but has a similar project.
- The other, however, loves the script and would like to bring it to Sony, with whom they have an overall deal. One territory (studio) officially covered.
- Repeat dose of Ambien from night before; find that butterflies have intensified. Double dose. Sleep.

Wednesday

- Receive late morning phone call from agent and manager; a cluster of passes, to be expected, but also some enthusiasm; several producers are fighting for territories.
- Your agent and manager assign out all the studios to the producers they feel have the best shot of setting the script up at those territories.
- The one or two territories that aren't covered are given to two different producers who have responded especially passionately to the script; they now have two territories.
- Your agent schedules some "meet and greets" with producers who liked your writing but passed on the script for various reasons.
- Sleep a bit better, thanks to the validation the script has received, completely unaware that the real anxiety has only just begun.

Thursday

- Agent and manager call in the morning: two studios passed. Before you get too dispirited, they remind you that the passes always come quickly and that there are still five other territories.
- Sure enough, that afternoon an enthusiastic call comes in from a vice president at Paramount. She's putting the script on the president's overnight read... a great sign.
- Two hours later, two more passes but another enthusiastic read from V.P. at Warner Brothers, who's also putting the script on the overnight read.
- Add Valium to your dose of Ambien. Sleep like a baby.

Friday

- Agent and manager call late morning. The script is now an official hot item, as both Paramount and Warner Brothers want to buy it.
- Spend the rest of the day on the phone with your agent, manager, and lawyer, who has now entered the fray to negotiate the deal.
- Paramount winds up winning, and the terms of your high six-figure deal are agreed to.
- Prepare for avalanche of meetings and announcement in the industry trade magazines (*Variety*, *Hollywood Reporter*).

Remember that the above is based on the experience of a script that actually sold. Most don't, which will mean that instead of the nice buttoned-up ending on Friday, things will drag on for weeks as your agent continues to try to breathe life into the script (sometimes they pull out a miracle; more often than not they don't, though you should hardly blame them). There are even better case scenarios in which scripts have gone out on a Tuesday and have sold by Wednesday morning. For the most part, however, the fact remains that the first forty-eight hours determines a script's fate; you will absolutely know from the town's response to the script if it's hot or not.

About the Author

David Kukoff is a screenwriter and television producer who lives in Thousand Oaks, California. He has over ten produced television and film credits to his name, has developed projects for every major studio, and is currently Vice President of Creative Affairs for Los Angeles-based JTN Productions. Mr. Kukoff is a faculty guest lecturer at UCLA where he teaches a weekly screenwriting course, and is on the board of directors at The Writer's Arc, a not-for-profit screenwriting fellowship organization.

Final Analysis

There is probably no profession more difficult to break into, and stay in, than that of a professional screenwriter. The jobs are few and far between, and you are always hopping from one to another with little – if any – assurance of stability. But if you have decided that this is the profession for you, that you have always wanted to be a voice in the world of film, then you owe it to yourself to take a pragmatic, almost scientific approach to what makes the wheels of the industry turn. And if you approach it with honesty, humility, and of course, a smidgen of talent to boot, you will find that it can be done. And if you do succeed, remember the adage that the person who loves what he does never works a day in his life, couldn't be more true.